THE BREAD & ROSES PLAYWRITING AWARD

The Bread & Roses Playwriting Award

Hungerland
by Rachel O'Regan,

I and the Village
by Darren Donohue,

Who You Are and
What You Do
by Hugh Dichmont

WINNING PLAYS - VOLUME I

www.breadandrosestheatre.co.uk

Hungerland © Rachel O'Regan
I and the Village © Darren Donohue
Who You Are and What You Do © Hugh Dichmont

First published by **The Bread & Roses Theatre** in 2022.

All rights reserved. No part of this book may be reproduced in any manner whatsoever without written permission, except in the case of brief quotations embodied in critical articles and reviews.

Design/Editing: Tessa Hart

ISBN 978-1-912504-08-4 (print)
ISBN 978-1-912504-09-1 (e-book)

Amateur and Professional Performing Rights

No performance of any kind of this play may be given unless a licence has been obtained, including excerpts and readings. Application should be made before rehearsals begin. Publication of these plays does not indicate availability for performance. This applies to all mediums and all languages.
To enquire about availability for performing rights and the necessary steps to undertake to obtain a licence, please contact info@breadandrosestheatre.co.uk in the first instance.

Contents

Hungerland — 1

I and the Village — 134

Who You Are and What You Do — 281

About the Playwrights & Theatre — 407

Special Thank You to

- All readers of the Playwriting Award
- Battersea & Wandsworth Trades Union Council (BWTUC)
- The Bread & Roses Pub
- Royal Victoria Hall Foundation
- Unity Theatre Trust
- Lambeth Council
- Arts Council England (Culture Recovery Fund)
- All individual donors & supporters

without whom the numerous steps towards the Playwriting Award, the production and the publication of these plays would not have been possible.

Hungerland

by Rachel O'Regan

"Why, sometimes I've believed as many as six impossible things before breakfast."

Lewis Carroll

For more information and support

beateatingdisorders.org.uk

Help for England
Helpline: 0808 801 0677
Email: help@beateatingdisorders.org.uk

Help for Scotland
Helpline: 0808 801 0432
Email: Scotlandhelp@beateatingdisorders.org.uk

Help for Wales
Helpline: 0808 801 0433
Email: waleshelp@beateatingdisorders.org.uk

Help for Northern Ireland
Helpline: 0808 801 0434
Email: NIhelp@beateatingdisorders.org.uk

Cast & Creatives

Hungerland by Rachel O'Regan was first performed at The Bread & Roses Theatre from 29th October to 9th November 2019, with the following cast and creatives:

<u>Cast:</u>

NICOLE
Odera Ndujiuba

ALICE
Tomi Jatto

MIKE
Matthew Wright

Creatives:

Directors
Rebecca Pryle & Velenzia Spearpoint

Assistant Director
Nathalie Wright

Producer
Ella Gamble

Assistant Producer
Tim Blore

Set & Costume Designer
Katie Lynch

Lighting & Sound Designer / Operator
Patrick Medway

Stage Manager
Zazie Rothfuchs

Creative Producer
Tessa Hart

Characters

ALICE

NICOLE

MIKE

ACT I: Down the Rabbit-Hole

We're in the kitchen. It's nice, well-sized, if a little too modernly furnished. On either side of the stage are two doors – one is the front door, and the other leads off to the rest of the house... bedroom, living area, bathroom and so on. NICOLE, *27, is standing at the kitchen bench, wearing a simple black dress and heels. Her hair is cropped short and practical. She stirs a pot of sauce, several cookbooks open in front of her. The mess is in stark contrast to the rest of the house, like it has a life of its own completely out of* NICOLE*'s control.*

NICOLE
This is it. Talk to me. Turn the heat up to high... sift in cornflour... oh, while whisking vigorously... and add a knob of butter. What? A knob is not a unit of measurement, Jamie. How much is a knob? How much? Shit. Mike, can you come out here for a second? Michael!

MIKE (off)
I still don't understand why we have to get so dressed up.

NICOLE
Of course you don't understand. You'd wear Crocs to our wedding if you could.

MIKE walks out from the bedroom, buttoning up a formal shirt. He's 27, tall and handsome – the kind of man you'd take home to your parents. But on his feet are a bright, hideous pair of Crocs.

MIKE
But they're so comfortable.

NICOLE
If you wear those at dinner, they're going in the blender.

MIKE
Sounds like someone has uncomfortable feet.

NICOLE
Shut up. I need your help. How big is a knob?

MIKE
Well... That depends on many factors. Temperature. Mood, certainly. Some say race is a factor but people get testy about that. It's a hairy subject.

He's proud of his joke, but NICOLE isn't impressed. At all.

NICOLE
A knob of butter. What is that, like a doorknob? That seems like a lot. This stupid cookbook is so bloody imprecise – a splash of cider, a glug of oil...

MIKE
Can't you just guesstimate?

NICOLE *darkens.*

NICOLE
You know how much I hate that word.

MIKE
Sorry, I forgot your fear of portmanteaus. What was the other one – spork.

NICOLE
Are you trying to kill me?

MIKE
And Brangelina. No, I think that's cute. We should have a couple name. Nicole and Mike. Nike! Goddess of shoes.

NICOLE
Stop being an idiot for a second and look at this gravy.

He peers at the gravy intently for a moment.

MIKE
Yep, that looks like gravy.

NICOLE
But does it look like the picture? I don't think it's thick enough, see. I need to increase the viscosity.

MIKE
You're increasing my viscosity.

NICOLE
What does that mean?

MIKE
No idea.

NICOLE
You're not helping.

MIKE
It's not a big deal. This dinner looks delicious and the rest? Well, it's just gravy, babe.

NICOLE
Goddamn it, Mike, what have I told you? Look at me. Am I an infant?

MIKE
No.

NICOLE
Am I an American baseball player from the Twenties?

MIKE
No.

NICOLE
Am I a talking pig? Don't answer that.

MIKE
It's no fun if you're just throwing them out there.

NICOLE
I am not your babe.

MIKE
I'm sorry. I just think if you're going to go to so much effort to make the perfect Christmas dinner you could have at least invited people to enjoy it with us.

NICOLE
And who is it you want to invite? Our friends?

MIKE
Well, maybe.

NICOLE
Our family?

MIKE
It could be nice.

NICOLE
Michael!

MIKE
I just want to get to know the people who know you. I haven't even met your parents yet.

NICOLE
There's plenty of time for that. But what you're talking about – families at Christmas. You never told me you were into S & M.

MIKE
I'm not! If you're not? Are you?

NICOLE *ignores him, going back to whisk her gravy.*

NICOLE
First, you have to try and cook enough for everyone and guaranteed there'll be someone with "dietary requirements". You're all squished around a table, pretending to be interested in each others' "careers" and "kids" and laughing at stupid jokes that come out of crackers. I am not wearing a paper hat, Mike. I just won't do it.

MIKE
All right, Scrooge McDuck.

NICOLE
Before you know it, someone would have suggested we play a game.

MIKE
Come on, games are the best part of Christmas! Everyone sat round the table, playing Revel Roulette.

NICOLE
God, do I ask?

MIKE
You know, Revels, the chocolate. They all look the same but have different fillings, orange, caramel, coffee –

NICOLE
I know what they are.

MIKE
And everyone has a favourite flavour and one they can't stand – raisin.

NICOLE (*At the same time*)
Raisin.

MIKE
So you empty out the bag in the middle of the table and close your eyes and eat a Revel and if you get your favourite flavour, you get another turn, but if you get the worst flavour, you have to skip a go and around and around you go until someone eats the last Revel.

NICOLE
And what do they win?

MIKE
At life, Nicole.

NICOLE
So, the game is just eating a bag of chocolate. That's stupid.

MIKE
Sometimes I think you just don't like fun.

NICOLE
Now, don't go back in there to play video games.

MIKE
But they're my present!

NICOLE
And I'm already severely regretting it. I need you to run me an errand. I forgot to get ice.

MIKE
Ice? What for?

NICOLE
To put the champagne in?

MIKE
Champagne?

He notices the bottle.

MIKE
Cristal? That's like two-hundred quid a bottle.

NICOLE
And I deserve it.

MIKE
You deserve a lot of things. We can't afford this.

NICOLE
I didn't work my arse off at law school to drink Lambrini. Ice. Michael.

MIKE
Nothing's open anyway.

NICOLE
Go to the off-licence down the road. They're Indian.

MIKE
Bangladeshi.

NICOLE
It doesn't matter.

MIKE
I'm sure it does to the Mojumdars.

NICOLE
How do you know their name?

MIKE
I talk to people with actual words that come out of my mouth.

NICOLE
Whatever, the point is they don't celebrate Christmas. So go and get the ice.

MIKE *picks up the car keys defeatedly.*

MIKE
Be back soon, babe.

MIKE *exits. We see the flash of headlights and hear the crunch of gravel as he rolls out of the driveway.* NICOLE *goes back to her gravy. She looks at the book, shrugs, and throws in the whole stick of butter.*

NICOLE
I hate Jamie Oliver.

As she is stirring in cornflour, a ringtone sounds. NICOLE *pulls her phone from her pocket and looks at the caller. She hesitates before ignoring the call. She pours herself a glass of champagne and opens the oven and gives the turkey another glaze. The next moments are a blur of* NICOLE *getting ready, pulling on a pair of pantyhose, applying lipstick in a mirror. All the while, smoke begins to rise from the oven. By the time she emerges in a red dress, it has filled the kitchen. There is a crunch of gravel and a flash of headlights at the driveway.*

NICOLE
What the hell is he doing back so early?

The smoke alarm goes off.

NICOLE
Shit! Shit shit shit.

NICOLE *tries to take the turkey out with her bare hands.*

NICOLE
Argh! You motherfucker.

She grabs a tea towel tries in vain to lift the turkey. The house is filling with smoke. She opens the front door to let it out, but it's not working fast enough. She runs back to the kitchen to grab a tea towel and fans smoke out the front door.

NICOLE
Bloody arsehole smoke alarm! Shut up, shut up!

At the doorway, ALICE *appears. She is 27 but looks younger, wearing a red coat. She carries a cloth bag. She stands, bewildered, sniffing at the air.* NICOLE *fans the smoke out the door, right into* ALICE's *face.*

NICOLE
Get... the fuck... out!

The smoke alarm dies, leaving the two of them frozen in silence.

ALICE
It's nice to see you, too, Nicole.

NICOLE
Jesus Christ. Jesus Christ.

ALICE
No, it's just me. Alice.

NICOLE
Alice. It is you.

ALICE
Who were you expecting, the ghost of Christmas past?

NICOLE
What the hell are you doing here? That came out wrong. What I mean is, how did you get this address? I've only just moved in.

ALICE
I asked Courtney.

NICOLE *is straightening up now, regaining her composure.*

NICOLE
Well, you should have called.

ALICE
I called so many times. You don't answer your phone.

NICOLE
Right, I had to change numbers. Bloody O2, you know.

ALICE
And email, that's down, too?

NICOLE
I have a new one, for work.

ALICE
Of course. And I suppose you didn't get any letters either?

NICOLE
Nobody sends letters, Alice.

ALICE
No, of course not. Facebook?

NICOLE
Alice, when did you get out? You didn't escape, did you? I don't want the police on my doorstep again.

ALICE
You make me sound like a criminal. No, it was totally by the book. You'd be proud, of how by the book it was, I mean.

NICOLE
They let you out?

ALICE
Just in time for the holidays.

NICOLE
This isn't like last time when you put rolls of coins in your underwear? Or when you drank eight litres of water?

ALICE
No, I learned from that the hard way. What goes in must come out. What goes down must come up.

NICOLE
What is that, an anorexic proverb?

ALICE
Physics. Plus they placed me on permanent watch for peeing all over the doctor's office.

NICOLE
Alice!

ALICE
I couldn't have stayed there even if I wanted to. Apparently I'm not sick enough.

NICOLE
I have to say you look... you look a lot better than the last time I saw you. You look well.

It's not the answer ALICE *is looking for. She collects herself.*

ALICE
And you... you look totally different. That dress! And what on earth have you done to your hair?

NICOLE
It's chic.

ALICE
It's short.

She reaches out to touch it, but NICOLE *pulls away.*

ALICE
What would Dad say?

NICOLE
That's the point, he doesn't get to.

ALICE
Oh, but he used to love our long hair.

NICOLE
And the matching outfits.

ALICE *tries to touch her hair again.*

ALICE
I just can't get used to it.

NICOLE
You're one to talk about changing appearances. God, look at the pair of us. We never could convince people we were twins, now there's no hope.

ALICE
Fraternal twins. The only thing we've ever shared is a womb.

NICOLE
Ugh, please, Alice.

ALICE
I was worried I'd soon forget what you looked like.

ALICE *reaches out to hug* NICOLE. *But* NICOLE *just stands there frozen. She's so taken aback that* ALICE *is able to slip past her into the house.* NICOLE *chases after her, removing an engagement ring she is wearing and slipping it in her pocket.*

NICOLE
No, wait, Alice –

ALICE
My goodness.

NICOLE
I'm not really prepared for visitors.

ALICE
Do you really live here?

NICOLE
Alice –

ALICE
How much is this place costing you to rent?

NICOLE
It's just a little house.

ALICE
In London. Which kidney did you sell? None? I chose the wrong career.

NICOLE
I'm sure you'd earn plenty if you had graduated med school. Alice, I'm sorry, I am happy to see you but–

ALICE *has produced a small box wrapped in tissue.*

ALICE
Merry Christmas. They were really out of gift options at the off- license, but they were the only shop open. Nice people, the Mojumdars.

NICOLE
What?

ALICE
They even gift-wrapped it for me in serviettes.

NICOLE *unwraps the gift.*

NICOLE
It's a box of tampons.

ALICE
At least *you'll* get some use out of them. I'm trying to be funny.

NICOLE
It's not even my size. Never mind that, Alice, you can't just drop in like this.

ALICE
What are you trying to say? There's no room at the inn? I can sleep on the sofa. I'll sleep on the floor if I have to. As long I can't be strapped into it, it's an upgrade.

NICOLE *does not like this kind of humour.*

NICOLE (*firmly*)
Alice.

ALICE
I have nowhere else to go, Nic.

NICOLE
What about Mum's? Does she even know you're here?

ALICE
I'm not a kid, I don't have to tell her where I'm going.

NICOLE
But don't you think she'll get a shock when she goes to visit you and you're not there? I'm calling her.

ALICE
Please don't. I will call her. I just can't go back to Mum's, please.

NICOLE
Why not?

ALICE
Have you met Mum?

NICOLE
Well, you can't stay here.

ALICE
Come on, I'll wash dishes and everything.

NICOLE
You won't make dishes to be washed. Alice, do you remember the last time we lived together? Do you really want that to happen again?

ALICE
I'm better now.

NICOLE
So you keep saying.

ALICE
I'll do anything, name your price. What do I have to do?

NICOLE
You know what you have to do.

ALICE
Fine.

NICOLE
Fine. Food's this way.

NICOLE *leads* ALICE *into the kitchen. She begins to cut into the turkey.*

NICOLE
Christ! It's ruined. I've ruined it. Incredible! It's still raw in the middle.

ALICE
You're cooking.

NICOLE
I'm glad that's what I appear to be doing.

ALICE
But you hate cooking.

NICOLE
I don't! How would you know? It's not like you were hanging around the kitchen.

ALICE
And there's so much of it too. Oh, God, I'm thick as gravy. I'm sorry.

NICOLE
What are you apologising for?

ALICE
Gatecrashing your party. How I could think you wouldn't have plans on Christmas day, I mean, you do have friends–

NICOLE
I do. But I'm not having a party.

ALICE
Then, who is all this food for?

NICOLE
Well, it's for me.

ALICE
What, all of it?

NICOLE
I'm not going to eat it all in one go.

ALICE
No, that would be crazy.

NICOLE
I must say. It's almost like you expected to find me sitting in my pyjamas eating cold KFC straight out of the bucket.

ALICE
I'm just surprised is all.

NICOLE
I'm allowed to do things that make *me* happy. Dad died a long time ago, it's no use sulking about it. Trust me, I've been there, done that. Bought the fucking fridge magnet.

ALICE
But it has been difficult?

NICOLE *has revealed too much. She collects herself.*

NICOLE
So the turkey is ruined but you can have a potato. Here, I cooked them in duck-fat.

ALICE
Nicole, actually, the reason I came here is to do with Dad. I know you've been taking care of his things while I've been sick. And I'm so grateful, really. But now that I'm better, I think this would be a good time for me to have a fresh start. Do you think you could talk to the bank about releasing my half of the insurance money?

NICOLE *begins to answer but there is a flash at the window and crunching of gravel outside.*

NICOLE
Oh, shit, he's back. You have to go.

ALICE
What? Who's back?

NICOLE
Mike. Quick, you go around the back.

ALICE
Why? Who's Mike?

NICOLE
My boyfriend. Don't look like that people have boyfriends. Normal people.

ALICE
Not you.

NICOLE *tries to physically push* ALICE *towards the door.*

NICOLE
Go, go. No, stop. He's coming up, you'd better hide in my room.

ALICE
What?

NICOLE
Just hide in the closet or under the bed, you'll fit. Come on, I'll let you know when it's safe to come out.

ALICE
Safe? Nic, what's going on?

NICOLE
Hurry!

ALICE
Why are you hiding me?

The front door swings open. MIKE *is carrying a bag of ice and a packet of Revels. He stares at* ALICE, *who is still wearing her red coat and carrying her sack of belongings.*

MIKE
I know they were putting Santa on a diet, but this is ridiculous.

NICOLE
Mike, Mike. This is my friend. Alice. From uni.

MIKE
Enchanté. What are you doing in my house?

NICOLE
She's not staying long, she just wanted to pop in and say Merry Christmas.

ALICE
Merry Christmas.

NICOLE
Okay, bye.

MIKE
Have we met before?

A beat as ALICE *is overcome with the sadness of this:*

ALICE
No.

MIKE
You look kind of familiar.

NICOLE
You have absolutely no connection.

MIKE
Well, any friend of Nicole's is - actually I've never met a friend of Nicole's.

ALICE
You're joking.

MIKE
What brings you to our neck of suburbia?

NICOLE
She's travelling. And she's just going back to her hotel.

ALICE
Hostel, actually.

MIKE
Hostel? You don't look like an Australian backpacker. You're not spending Christmas with family or... ?

ALICE
No, I get the strangest feeling I wouldn't be welcome.

MIKE
Fuck, sorry. So what are your Christmas plans?

ALICE
I don't have any.

MIKE
You should have Christmas dinner with us.

He says this casually as he crams his face with Revels.

ALICE
Really?

NICOLE
Yeah, really?

ALICE
I shouldn't, I'd be imposing.

NICOLE
I've already set the table, Mike.

MIKE
It's no problem. Come on, you can't spend Christmas alone in a hostel, can she Nicole? Think of the baby Jesus.

NICOLE
You're not religious.

MIKE
I dabble.

ALICE
Well, only if you're sure it's not a bother.

MIKE
There's just one condition – you have to help me eat all of this delicious food Nicole's made.

NICOLE *has a light bulb moment.*

NICOLE
Yes. That's the rule.

ALICE *knows* NICOLE *is challenging her.*

ALICE
Thank you. Thank you.

NICOLE
Well. There's a bathroom through that door, on the left. You can wash up in there.

ALICE goes to do so. NICOLE claps her hands to her face.

NICOLE
Oh my God... What are you eating?

MIKE
Revels.

NICOLE
We're about to have dinner, I can't believe you!

NICOLE tips the ice into the sink and puts the champagne in to chill.

MIKE
Don't turn this around on me. I leave this house for five minutes
   and you've gone and made a friend.

NICOLE
I can explain.

MIKE
Where did you find her? She's kind of hot, in a Keira Knightley sort of way, if you know what I mean. She has no tits.

NICOLE
Oh, my God. Please don't talk about her tits. She's an old, old friend from university. I didn't even know she was coming, believe me, or I would have stopped her. She's one of those people who just attract chaos. And now you've gone and invited her to dinner.

MIKE
She seems nice enough.

ALICE *enters the room again. She is blinking back tears as if she has just had a quick cry.*

MIKE
So, Alice, is it? What do you do for a living? Let me guess – you're a model.

ALICE
Oh, no!

NICOLE
He tries that line on all the ladies.

MIKE
No, I don't.

ALICE
Actually, I'm sort of just taking a break.

NICOLE
Travelling, she's travelling.

MIKE
Oh, have you been anywhere exotic?

ALICE
Well most recently, I finished a long stay in Solihull.

NICOLE *laughs.*

NICOLE
Oh Alice, you're so funny.

ALICE, *weirded out, turns to* MIKE.

ALICE
What do you do?

MIKE
I'm a lawyer, like Nicole.

ALICE
Oh! I never would have guessed it from the footwear.

NICOLE
GET THEM OFF NOW.

MIKE *obeys and leaves the room.* NICOLE *busies herself with putting out another table setting.*

ALICE
University friend?

NICOLE
I panicked.

ALICE
So you two live together, it's serious?

NICOLE
It's always serious.

ALICE
But you haven't told him about me, your long-lost twin?

NICOLE
Believe it or not, it's never come up.

ALICE
So bring it up.

NICOLE
Isn't that what *you're* good at?

ALICE *is visibly wounded by the remark as* MIKE *reappears in a pair of sad black dress shoes. But on his head is a paper hat.*

MIKE
Better? May I take your coat, Alice?

ALICE
Thanks, but I'd rather keep it on. Cold hands, warm heart and all that.

MIKE
Are you sure? It can get quite stuffy in here with the oven going.

NICOLE
She's fine, Mike.

ALICE
How did you two meet?

MIKE
Job interview. We were both going for the same role. Of course, Nicole got it. I found another firm down the road. We kept bumping into each other at Pret. It was a sign.

NICOLE
Because Pret is such a rare lunch spot for office workers.

MIKE
But it was *our* Pret. Can you imagine if I'd went to the other one across the road?

NICOLE
Yes, I would have met someone else.

MIKE
See, she doesn't believe in destiny.

NICOLE
No, I believe in making things happen for yourself. The moment you believe your future is written in the stars is when you stop taking responsibility for it.

ALICE
And luck has nothing to do with it?

NICOLE
Four leaf clovers and fortune cookies?

ALICE
Say there were two siblings, twins in fact. Same upbringing, identical lifestyles but just one of them gets sick. That seems like fate to me.

NICOLE
But it's as you say, if they had the same upbringing, the same opportunities, then one must have done something.

ALICE
Done what, exactly.

Beat. MIKE, *sensing the awkwardness in the room, claps his hands.*

MIKE
Is anyone else hungry?

NICOLE
Right. Grab a plate and help yourselves. I'm afraid the turkey is stuffed in more ways than one, but there's still all the trimmings.

MIKE grabs a plate and heads to the kitchen bench. NICOLE follows. ALICE stands awkwardly to the side, still wearing her coat with her cloth bag hanging off her shoulder.

MIKE
This looks amazing, babe. Come on, dig in, Alice.

NICOLE
Remember your deal.

ALICE picks up a plate and walks over to the bench. She adds a couple of sprouts to her plate. MIKE has already piled his high.

MIKE
You gotta eat more than that. It's not Christmas until someone has to roll you out the door.

ALICE adds some carrots and parsnips.

MIKE
Here, you gotta try some of Nicole's gravy.

ALICE
No, thanks, I'm okay.

MIKE
Come on, it's homemade.

ALICE
I'm vegan.

MIKE
GET OUT.

NICOLE
It was nice of you to stop by.

MIKE
I'm sorry, it's not that I'm offended at your existence. I just couldn't trust someone who chooses to not eat cheese. It's freakish.

ALICE
I think it's freakish that humans are the only species on earth that consumes another animal's milk.

NICOLE
Okay, no. We are not having a vegan argument on Christmas. And Jesus, by the way, ate meat.

ALICE
He also starved himself in the desert for forty days, what's your point?

NICOLE *responds by picking up her plate and walking to the dining room table.*

MIKE
Now, whatever you do, just say the food's good if you want to get out alive.

MIKE and ALICE take their seats at the table. ALICE and NICOLE are sat on opposite ends, with MIKE facing out towards the audience. Immediately, MIKE digs in to the meal. From on now all his lines are said with a mouth full of food.

MIKE
Babe, this gravy has the perfect viscosity.

NICOLE
The trick was cornflour.

NICOLE starts eat to while watching ALICE, who is looking down at her plate as if she doesn't know what to do with it.

ALICE
Could I please have some water?

NICOLE pours ALICE a glass, but instead ALICE takes the pitcher and pours out a glass, drinks, then pours out another.

MIKE
Thirsty?

NICOLE
Careful you don't ruin your appetite.

MIKE
So, old university friends. You two must be close.

NICOLE (*in unison*)
You could say that.

ALICE (*in unison*)
You could say that.

MIKE
Wow, really close. Now, it's your duty to tell me what kind of crazy things Nic got up to in her uni days.

NICOLE
Michael, honestly.

MIKE
Come on Alice. Were there parties, drugs, boys?

ALICE
I'm sorry to disappoint you. Nicole was very focused on her studies.

NICOLE
Haven't I told you I'm practically perfect in every way?

MIKE
But there must have been one drunk night when she completely lost her shit.

NICOLE
Really, we're trying to eat. Look at Alice, she hasn't even touched her meal.

All eyes on ALICE *now, as she pushes the food around on her plate.*

ALICE
Although, there was one night.

MIKE
I knew it!

NICOLE
Alice.

ALICE
We'd just finished our final exams.

NICOLE
Don't.

ALICE
So we thought we'd go down to Brighton for the summer. I practically had to force Nicole to come with us because she wanted to get ahead of her reading for the next term.

MIKE
Story checks out.

ALICE
But once we got there, you tried to deny it at first, but you had the best time. Something happened to you out there. It was like you didn't give a shit anymore. We just sat around and read classic novels and ate fish and chips and smoked pot. Then that last night, we went down to the

beach to get ice-cream and there was this stoner van with graffiti of naked girls all over it and a surfboard on the top. So Nicole runs down in her bikini to the driver, who's sitting in there watching the waves come in and says, "Can I have a go?". No, the waves are too rough. "I didn't mean out there." And suddenly she's climbed up the top of his van and she's standing on the top of his surfboard and he starts driving down the promenade fast, laughing like a maniac, and we're all screaming, me and the girls and everyone, "Get down, you're going to fall, you're going to die!".

MIKE
And? What happened next?

ALICE
The van stopped. Nicole got down. The next morning we took a train home and she started the first book on her holiday reading list.

MIKE
Poo.

NICOLE
Sorry to disappoint.

MIKE (*clasping* ALICE*'s hand*)
Come on, you must have a better story than that. Think back to freshers – hey, what happened to your knuckles?

ALICE *draws her hand away and rolls down her sleeve.*

ALICE
I used to have this cat.

MIKE
Say no more. Did you know cats are the only self-domesticated animal? They saw humans had food and shelter and chose to live with us, they invaded. It's why they're so evil, they're basically colonisers.

NICOLE
See, I respect that. It's survival of the fittest. They know what they want and how to get it. And you always know where you stand with a cat. Dogs on the other hand, they're so needy they love you even if you treat them like shit.

MIKE
I want to get a dog.

NICOLE
So we can have double the fur-shedding and bad smells?

MIKE
I was thinking a little warmth and companionship.

NICOLE
You're right. We should get a dog. If we're lucky, maybe he'll have a taste for Crocs.

MIKE
I hope he does. So I can buy more Crocs. In all the colours of the rainbow.

ALICE *laughs.*

ALICE
You two fight like siblings.

MIKE
As long as we keep it personal and not professional, right babe?

ALICE
What do you mean?

MIKE
Nicole is a prosecutor while I defend the innocent.

NICOLE
And the guilty.

ALICE
So if I wanted to sue someone, which of you would I hire?

NICOLE
What have you done?

ALICE
I haven't done anything. I'm a victim – we're all victims, of the way the media talks about women's bodies.

NICOLE
Christ.

MIKE
I'm afraid you can't just sue the media. It's an entity, you might as well try and sue God. And even He might not have as much power as Rupert Murdoch.

ALICE
True, silly me. But what if you had a blatantly awful publication, something truly, noxiously dangerous that you could make an example of? Then all the other publications would fall in line.

She reaches into her bag and pulls out a tabloid.

MIKE
"Beached: Top Ten Worst Celebrity Bikini Bodies".

ALICE
See, I think if you could scrape together enough articles like that from one shitty tabloid, we could have a real case. A class action. All we'd have to do is show that these journalists are telling young impressionable girls that they're worthless without the perfect body. That being skinny is the ultimate goal and you should stop at nothing to achieve it.

MIKE
Sorry, what page is that on?

ALICE
Every page! It's all there, if you read between the lines.

NICOLE *scoffs.*

ALICE
Is something funny?

NICOLE
A court deals with evidence, Alice, not emotions. But besides that, let's the say we can objectively prove this and, landmark case, we take away the freedom of the press. Can you honestly say the problem would stop? These – people... with eating disorders... they look for this kind of material. If you shut down one magazine, they'd just find another one. Or make a website dedicated to those kinds of images. You can practically remove them from society, put them in a hospital where the only thing they have to look at is drywall and they will still starve themselves.

MIKE
You seem to know a lot about this.

ALICE
Yeah, you do.

NICOLE
All I'm saying is, it hardly seems fair to penalise the media for something that's beyond their control. It would be like banning knives because someone might cut themselves or banning bleach in case somebody drinks it.

ALICE
Except knives are also used for cooking. Bleach gets stains out of your clothes. Tell me what use, what benefit,

what use an article about the worst celebrity beach bodies is for anyone.

MIKE
Alice, darling, have you ever thought of going into law?

ALICE
Medicine was my thing. Do you know the most important rule of medicine? First, do no harm.

NICOLE
Except when it comes to yourself, right?

MIKE *stands up.*

MIKE
I think it's time for a mood lightener. Who's up for a game of Revel Roulette?

NICOLE
We're still eating. In fact, Alice, your dinner's getting cold.

ALICE
What's Revel Roulette?

He has pulled out the bag of Revels.

MIKE
So, they all look the same but they have different fillings, orange, caramel, coffee –

ALICE
I know what they are.

MIKE
And everyone has a favourite flavour and one they can't stand. So if you get your favourite flavour, you get another turn, but if you get the worst flavour, you have to skip, and you play until the bag is eaten.

ALICE
What if you don't like Revels at all?

MIKE
God, you two should be related.

NICOLE
Michael, for Christ's sake, and I do mean literally, is it too much to ask for a simple, civilised Christmas dinner?

Silence falls around the table.

MIKE
Sorry.

Everyone picks up their cutlery. MIKE and NICOLE start to eat. ALICE begins to cut up her food into smaller and smaller bites, until it's almost a mush on her plate. Her vision tunnels in on her plate and her chest begins to rise and fall as she's aware NICOLE is watching her and it won't be long before she is exposed to MIKE too. All the while, MIKE and NICOLE are making excruciating small talk.

MIKE
It's cold outside.

NICOLE
Freezing.

MIKE
Lucky we have good heating.

NICOLE
It's been a cold December.

MIKE
So rare to see that kind of snow in London.

NICOLE
Nothing compared to up north though.

MIKE
Oh no. Not at all. Snow... is cold.

NICOLE
See, isn't this better?

She reaches out to pet MIKE's *hand. He notices that her ring is missing.*

MIKE
Where's your ring, babe?

NICOLE
Hm?

MIKE
You never take your ring off.

ALICE *snaps out of her reverie.*

ALICE
Ring?

NICOLE
Does anyone want tea?

MIKE
It's not tea-time, we're still eating dinner.

NICOLE
It's always tea–time. I fucking love tea, don't you?

ALICE
Are... are you two engaged?

NICOLE
I had to take it off to stuff the turkey, alright?

She takes the ring out of her pocket and puts it on.

NICOLE
Bloody hell.

ALICE
When were you going to tell me?

NICOLE
Alice, come on.

ALICE
You could have sent me a letter, for God's sake.

MIKE
Don't get upset. Sometimes estranged university friends don't tell each other everything. Nic hasn't even told her folks.

NICOLE
Mike. I was going to tell you, Alice.

ALICE
When?

NICOLE
I don't know, over coffee–

ALICE
When did Mike propose?

MIKE
Oh no, it was really all Nicole's doing. She had it all planned out. We went down to Sloane Square to have lunch at this really posh French restaurant, bloody hell it cost me, you know you pay like 30 quid for an entrée and they bring

you like a cube of soup. But they had his thing called foie gras, it's this fatty liver they get from force-fed ducks and it tastes really evil but also ah- mazing and –

ALICE
Yeah, yeah, not important –

MIKE
On the way back to the tube, we walked past Tiffany's and Nic pulled me over, pointed to a diamond ring in the window and said, "You see that? You're going to walk inside and buy that ring and when you come out, I'll say yes to anything you ask me." So I went inside, pointed out to the clerk the ring I wanted, bought it and when I came outside, I got down on one knee and said, "Can I buy a pool table?".

NICOLE
I'd never been so embarrassed. People were pointing, clapping.

MIKE
I had to make you fight for it a little. I always say Nic's the only girl I know capable of proposing to herself. I'm just an accessory.

NICOLE (*admiring the ring*)
But it's a beautiful accessory.

MIKE
And I'm still waiting on my pool table.

ALICE
I can't believe you're getting married.

NICOLE
What do you think?

ALICE
I think... I think he's really lovely, Nicole.

NICOLE
And?

ALICE
Congratulations, I guess! I'm happy for you, honestly.

MIKE
A toast!

NICOLE
Mike, fuck off.

MIKE
Come on, it's an occasion.

MIKE gets up and fetches the champagne from the sink. He pours three glasses.

MIKE
To my beautiful, smart, mad, maddening fiancée. May you always get your own way.

NICOLE
Cheers.

MIKE
Cheers.

ALICE
Cheers.

NICOLE *and* MIKE *drink.*

MIKE
Okay, I admit, this is better than Lambrini. You're not drinking, Alice.

ALICE
Sorry, I shouldn't have let you pour me a glass.

MIKE
You don't eat meat and you don't drink either? Are you human?

ALICE
You must think I'm mad.

MIKE
We're all mad here. But this is Cristal.

ALICE
I'm full.

MIKE
But you haven't touched your meal. It's not that bad.

NICOLE
Not that bad?

MIKE
Please take a sip.

ALICE *stares at the food and the champagne. She raises the glass to her lips – but breaks down in sobs.*

MIKE
What's wrong?

ALICE
I can't.

NICOLE
Don't be silly.

MIKE
What can't you do?

ALICE
I can't... I can't catch up.

MIKE
Catch up?

ALICE
I've missed everything.

ALICE tries to calm herself down.

ALICE
I'm sorry. It's just... I was away for so long... you know... travelling. It's like everyone's grown up without me, getting promoted or married or having babies and I'm a twenty-seven year old dropout with no qualifications, no career. I have nothing. I don't even know how to put my bed sheets on by myself. I've lost my adulthood.

NICOLE
Look, there's no point getting upset.

MIKE
Yeah, no-one knows how to put bed sheets on.

NICOLE
Alice. Look at me. I only got here through hard work. And you can too.

MIKE
You must be smart if you were studying medicine. How did you two meet each other if you were on different campuses?

NICOLE
You just have to suck it up a little. Start adulting.

ALICE
You're right. I can adult.

NICOLE
That's the spirit.

MIKE
And if it makes you feel any better, we're not normal either. Nobody buys a house at the age of twenty-seven.

Immediately NICOLE *tenses. Every bit of her body language is trying to tell* MIKE *to stop talking.*

ALICE
You mean rent.

NICOLE
Yes, Mike, we rent.

MIKE
Well, I suppose we rent from the bank. But they wouldn't have even looked at us for a mortgage if Nicole didn't have all that money for the down payment.

NICOLE
Shut up, Mike!

But he's already done the damage - and fades into the background as ALICE *turns on* NICOLE.

ALICE
You bought this house?

NICOLE
Mortgage. We got it at a very good rate.

ALICE springs up from the table – she's panicking, pacing. NICOLE remains in her chair, she hasn't even put down her cutlery.

ALICE
Oh my God.

MIKE
What's happening?

NICOLE
Calm down.

ALICE
How much?

NICOLE
Please sit down.

ALICE
HOW MUCH?

NICOLE
I still have a couple thousand left.

ALICE
Oh my God. Oh my God.

MIKE
I am very confused.

ALICE
Why?

NICOLE
We wouldn't have been able to mortgage the house without the deposit. It's a house in Zone 2, Alice, in a few years it will pay for itself.

ALICE is not listening. She is having a panic attack. MIKE gets up to help her. NICOLE puts down her cutlery but stays seated.

NICOLE
Calm down, Alice.

MIKE
What's wrong with her?

NICOLE
She always does this.

MIKE
Is she asthmatic?

NICOLE
Stop fussing over her, you'll just make it worse.

Suddenly ALICE is too consumed by rage to panic.

ALICE
How could you?

NICOLE
If you want to talk let's talk, but I'm not arguing with you like children.

ALICE
How could you do this to me? I'm your sister.

NICOLE *shakes her head in warning.*

MIKE
As in sorority sister?

ALICE
Do you know why it's called a trust? Because you're supposed to be able to trust the person holding the money.

NICOLE
Let's sit down and talk about it like adults.

ALICE
All the time I was in hospital, fighting for my life.

NICOLE
 Enough drama.

NICOLE
You were playing house with your pretend boyfriend -

MIKE
What the hell is going on?

ALICE *turns to him.*

ALICE
I'm Nicole's twin sister. She's been hiding me from you.

MIKE
How did this just become *EastEnders*? What?

NICOLE
Don't listen to her, she's blowing everything out of proportion - as usual.

ALICE
I've been struggling with an eating disorder for years -

NICOLE
Struggling, that's so passive –

ALICE
- for years. I barely saw you. Every time it was another excuse I thought, she's successful, she's moving on with her life, I can't begrudge her that. Not after she's gone out of her way to look after my finances after Dad died, only now I see why you were so desperate to get your claws on it. It's no wonder you rarely visited – you would have imploded from the guilt. You bitch!

Now MIKE *is on the defence.*

MIKE
Wait, wait, wait, wait. I don't know who the hell you *think* you are but you can't come in here, invite yourself over on Christmas day and attack my fiancée. Nicole might be cold sometimes but she's honest about who she is. She told me you were trouble and I should have believed her. I'm sorry, babe.

NICOLE
It's alright.

MIKE
And I'm sorry that you're unwell, quite obviously deluded, but that's no excuse to make up lies about Nicole's family. I think if you were so set on destroying her reputation you would have done your homework and found that Nicole's father is quite alive and well.

ALICE *looks to* NICOLE. *Shock, anger, pity.*

ALICE
Is there anything real about you?

NICOLE
Alice, I think we've had enough now.

ALICE
Our dad is dead. He died in a car accident three years ago.

MIKE
No, Nicole's dad is alive. Tell her, Nicole.

ALICE
Go on, just try. Tell me he's alive. Tell me!

NICOLE *can't even look* MIKE *in the eye.*

MIKE
Please.

NICOLE *shakes her head.* MIKE *grabs the nearest piece of furniture to lean on, white-knuckled.*

MIKE
Oh, my God. Your Dad's... he was going to walk you down the aisle, Nicole. Oh, my God. You lied to me.

NICOLE
I didn't lie. You never asked.

MIKE
Oh, that makes it okay then. I never specifically asked if your Dad was dead, because that's a natural thing to bring up in conversation.

NICOLE
Precisely.

MIKE
And what about her then? Did you also choose to omit those facts?

NICOLE
Oh, come on Mike. Don't pretend like your family is perfect. I've watched you. Your mother can barely be in the same room with you, you have so little in common. Your own father thinks you're a failure. You can't spend a day with him without getting in a screaming match. Is that what's so precious to you? The fighting, the drama. We're so above all of it. You and me, we're real, we don't need anybody else.

Beat.

MIKE
Did you really buy this house with stolen money?

NICOLE *realises she can't talk him back from this right now. She turns on*
ALICE *in a calm fury.*

NICOLE
Yes, I spent all your money. Is that what you want to hear? I spent it, while you withered away in hospital, I invested it in a future you'd opted out on, I made a decision based on logic and reason.

ALICE
It wasn't your decision to make. It was my money.

NICOLE
And what were you going to do with it? Spend it on diet pills and laxatives? On enemas and black market Ritalin?

It's been three years since Dad died and you're still carrying on with this bullshit. Police on my doorstep! Mum calling from the hospital, just breathing down the phone she can't speak for crying so hard. Everyone bending over backwards to help you but you're just determined to keep killing yourself for no reason. I don't see why I shouldn't keep the money. What use is it to someone who's already dead.

ALICE *is shell-shocked.* NICOLE *looks a little afraid of the words that have just fallen out of her mouth but she has remained calm throughout.*

ALICE
I'm going to be sick.

ALICE *runs for the bathroom, exits.* MIKE *gets up to follow her.*

NICOLE (*calling*)
Just don't use my toothbrush, sis.

MIKE
Aren't you going to do anything?

NICOLE
This is what she always does, she's desperate for attention.

MIKE
I don't believe you.

MIKE *begins to walk towards the bathroom.*

NICOLE
Do not follow her. If you validate this behaviour, it will only encourage her. This is how she gets what she wants.

MIKE
You're sick.

We hear ALICE *being sick.* MIKE *goes to tend to her.*

NICOLE
Don't you dare go to her, Michael.

MIKE *goes to tend to* ALICE *and exits.*

MIKE *(offstage)*
Are you okay?

NICOLE *steels herself, regains composure. Slowly, she picks up a knife and fork. She continues to eat, stone-faced, as her sister is violently ill in the bathroom.*

ACT II: Through the Looking Glass

Later: it's three in the morning. The still of cold. Fairy lights are still twinkling on the windows. The turkey is sitting untouched on the counter. As if in a trance, ALICE *enters dressed in a nightie, floating through the dark into the kitchen. She opens the fridge door and stands in the ghostly light. She looks at the food for a long a moment, picks up a Christmas cake and smells it.* ALICE's *shadow grows enormous behind her. She puts it back. Her shadow shrinks. She shakes herself out of it and closes the door.* ALICE *walks out. Time passes, carols swell and fade outside.* NICOLE *quietly pads through the kitchen in silk pyjamas. She opens the fridge and takes out a Christmas cake. She cuts a huge slice and begins to eat, standing over the sink.* ALICE *enters again, bleary-eyed.*

ALICE
Nic?

NICOLE *tries to sneak away quickly, but in her haste stubs her toe on the bench, hard. Cake crumbs spray from her mouth. She yelps in pain.*

NICOLE
Argh!

ALICE
Oh my God! What is it?

NICOLE
Ow, ow, ow, ow, ow!

The sounds come out strangled – it's the first time NICOLE *has outburst like this in front of her sister.* ALICE *turns on the lights.*

ALICE
Are you okay?

NICOLE
No! I've stubbed my toe! It's the worst pain in the world.

ALICE
Oh, shit. I can get you some ice.

NICOLE *bites down on her tears.*

NICOLE
Don't be ridiculous. It's just a stubbed toe. I'll be fine.

ALICE *goes to inspect the injury.*

ALICE
Let me see it. Oh, you've split the nail.

NICOLE
At least now I'm symmetrical. Bleeding from both ends.

She shows ALICE *her hands, blistered raw.*

ALICE
What happened to your hands?!

NICOLE I must have burnt them when I took the turkey out of the oven. I didn't even realise.

ALICE
That looks painful.

NICOLE
It's fine.

ALICE
I think you should go to hospital and get that looked at.

NICOLE
I'm not going to go to bloody hospital for every bloody problem in my life. ... Go back to bed, Alice. I'm sorry I woke you.

ALICE
It's alright, I wasn't really sleeping. I have these vivid dreams when I'm... anyway. What are you doing up?

NICOLE
We never actually got too much eating. I'm starving. I don't suppose you want any Christmas cake?

The mood has settled between them – NICOLE *is offering food now*
rather than forcing it.

ALICE
The rule is, cake tomorrow and cake yesterday — but never cake today.

NICOLE
What?

ALICE
Not at three in the morning.

NICOLE
Christ, is it? It's probably just as well, it tastes bloody awful. All plastic marzipan and dried fruit. Anything that lasts that long is not to be trusted.

ALICE
Then why are you eating it?

NICOLE
You can't have Christmas without Christmas cake.

NICOLE *eats the cake,* ALICE *watching intently.*

NICOLE
What?

ALICE
Nothing. Hm.

NICOLE
What? You know if I did this to you, you'd go batshit.

ALICE
Sorry. It's just... you just ate that cake without even thinking about the calories.

NICOLE
I hate to break it to you, but that's how most of us eat.

NICOLE *cuts herself a second slice.*

ALICE
I know, I'm jealous. Once you remember something like that it's hard to forget. Did you know the average person eats 6000 calories on Christmas day?

NICOLE
I'm not even hungry anymore.

NICOLE *puts down the slice, then shrugs and picks it up again.*

NICOLE
You always were annoyingly good at maths.

ALICE
I liked it. Maths brings order to a chaotic world. And numbers never lie.

NICOLE
That depends on how you look at them.

NICOLE gets a handful of ice and wraps it in a tea towel to press to her foot.

NICOLE
Can I ask you something?

ALICE
Okay.

NICOLE
Why do you do it?

ALICE
You really want to know?

NICOLE
I'm curious.

ALICE
Everyone is until they realise it's not glamorous or quirky or like bloody Cassie from *Skins*. If I tell you, it has to be the whole truth. Ugly and unfiltered. And you can't get upset.

NICOLE
Me, upset?

ALICE
You can't... disagree. You have to accept what I'm saying. I'm not lying or exaggerating, my reality is just different from yours. Even if it's not the truth, it's still my truth.

NICOLE
As a lawyer, there is so much wrong with that sentence.

ALICE
Will you listen?

NICOLE
You always say I don't understand you. So make me understand.

ALICE
It's hard. When I was in treatment, they kept harping on about finding the root cause. It's because you had a Barbie. Your mother used to diet. A boy called you fat once and it stuck to your ribs. But honestly I think I've always been this way, that it's just been lying dormant until –

NICOLE
Dad.

ALICE (*firm*)
I've told you it's not about that. Look, we don't ask people with cancer why they got sick. Did they do something

wrong? Is it society's fault? Are they just self-obsessed? No, we help them get on with it.

NICOLE
Maybe I'm asking the wrong question. What I want to know is, how?

ALICE
How?

NICOLE
Alice, don't play dumb. You studied medicine. You know the body needs food.

ALICE
I know. I eat. I do! Everyone seems to think we survive on black coffee and cigarettes. Of course we eat.

NICOLE
You know what I mean. Hunger is a survival instinct. Don't you feel it? I am a complete cow if I don't have breakfast first thing in the morning.

ALICE
Only when you don't have breakfast?

NICOLE
If you're not going to be serious...

ALICE
Alright, I'm sorry.

NICOLE
You know, food is also pleasure. It's meant to be enjoyed.

ALICE
I like food. A little too much actually, that's the problem.

NICOLE
Yeah, right.

ALICE
I dream about food.

NICOLE
Oh yeah? What kind?

ALICE
Mmm, celery and cabbage soup. I still have taste buds. I like what everyone does. Biscuits. Bad shit.

NICOLE
Bad?

ALICE
Stuff that will harden your arteries quicker than you can say Elvis. Krispy Kremes and cold leftover KFC and burgers. I can't tell you what I'd do if I had a really good, shitty burger. The ones with that sort of weird orange American cheese that doesn't melt.

NICOLE
Why's that?

ALICE
No clue. It's American, it's probably made of plastic.

NICOLE
What would happen if you had a burger?

ALICE
I don't know. It's the mess. Once you start eating a burger, once it's in your hands and dripping down your arms, it's too messy to stop and you have to keep going. And then you just ... keep going.

NICOLE
You feel the urge to binge.

NICOLE *is nodding, seeming to start to understand.*

ALICE
I know my triggers. *That's* a good thing.

NICOLE
And what about after, do you feel the urge to purge?

ALICE
God!

NICOLE
Alright.

ALICE
That sounds like an action movie.

NICOLE
Alright, you know I didn't mean to rhyme.

ALICE
Coming this summer, a woman must fight for her life in "The Urge to Purge". Starring Vin Diesel.

NICOLE
You're taking the piss.

ALICE
Alright. You want to know the truth? Sometimes, when I was bad, I'd sleep through the day just so I wouldn't feel the hunger pangs. But also, in a way, it sounds mad, but I started to like the feeling. Or just became addicted to it. It's a constant reminder of what you're doing to yourself, and it's telling you to keep going, keep going. But sometimes the pain is too loud and you have to give in. The voice goes away then and it's like it's given up on you. You'll do anything to get it back. That's the only way I can describe it.

NICOLE
A voice?

ALICE *(embarrassed)*
The girls at the clinic called it Ana.

NICOLE
Ana?

ALICE
Short for anorexia. Or Mia for bulimia. I know it sounds silly but it also makes sense. When it takes over you become someone you don't even recognise. Ana, Mia. That's why it's so hard to explain myself ... because I am not myself. You see.

NICOLE
Is that what it was like in the clinic?

ALICE
You would know if you ever visited.

NICOLE
I told you, I hate those places.

ALICE
Hospitals?

NICOLE
No, the Midlands.

ALICE *smiles.*

NICOLE
This is good, you back in the real world. Being with normal people again will straighten you out.

ALICE
Normal people like you?

NICOLE
Everyone. The girls will be thrilled. I'm sure. To be honest, we kind of lost touch.

ALICE
To be honest, so have I.

NICOLE
No! But we were only friends because we had you in common, they actually liked you. What happened?

ALICE
At first they visited every week. Promised to see me through it. But then I wasn't getting any better. I stopped getting visits. It's fine, I mean, eating disorders are super boring.

NICOLE
What about Courtney? She was so excited about doing some meditation retreat with you.

ALICE
Oh, fuck off.

NICOLE
Whoa.

ALICE
Sorry, I'm just sick to the back teeth of this New Age quackery. You know how white people get about yoga, like

it's the cure to cancer or something. And now she's vegan, ugh.

NICOLE
Aren't you vegan?

ALICE
Yeah, but I don't care about animals, it's different. For Courtney, veganism is just a gateway to wearing leggings as trousers. When I first got sick, she gave me this big speech about the healing powers of meditation. That all I had to do to solve my problems was listen to the voice within. Like I haven't been trying to shut off that voice for three years. But I tried, I went to a stupid class, I nearly choked to death on incense. And nothing. I just sat there thinking about what I would have for dinner, and what I wouldn't have for dinner, and my thighs and a million other different things and this one time my crush waved at me and I waved back and they were really waving at someone behind me.

NICOLE
What happened?

ALICE
I was explaining how I see myself, trying to explain anyway, and she started shouting. "Well, if you're really so huge then what am I?"

NICOLE
Medically obese.

ALICE
Nicole!

NICOLE
What? It's the truth. Everyone knows once this yoga thing gets old she'll be straight back on the Nando's. That girl has no handle on life.

ALICE
All I know is she completely invalidated my feelings. Turned it all
around on herself. Like *my* bad feelings were trying to make *her* feel bad. All that aside, I forgave her. I decided to be the bigger person.

NICOLE
Figuratively speaking.

ALICE
That's funny.

NICOLE
I'm here all week.

ALICE
No, you're doing the same thing she did.

NICOLE
What?

ALICE
I suppose I can't blame you, it's a female instinct.

NICOLE
Isn't that a little sexist?

ALICE
Don't take the moral high ground, Nic, it doesn't suit you. I may have taken a more politically correct stance at one time, I always try to give the benefit of the doubt, you try and see past the weird remarks and backhanded compliments. But when I lost weight it all became so obvious. Even you're doing it now, picking on Court's weight and don't get defensive - I'm not calling you out. It's in your nature. There's nothing more toxic than a woman faced with another woman.

NICOLE
Who are you and what have you done with my sweet little Alice?

ALICE
Can you honestly say you have never hated another woman because she's prettier than you or smarter than you or gets more attention? There we have it. Of course, it's different for me.

NICOLE
Is that so?

ALICE
I've never lost weight because of the way I looked, or the way someone else looked. It was never about that at all. But try telling women that. It goes against everything they've ever learnt.

NICOLE
Don't you think you're overgeneralising?

ALICE
Of course I am, I'm making a point. The same point I told Courtney: this is not about you. When I say I feel fat, I am talking only about myself. I am my only reference point, my body is the compass, you're not even on the map. It's not my fault if you get offended. But you can't talk about weight without every woman in the world trying to make it about herself.

NICOLE
Are you sure she wasn't just trying to empathise?

ALICE
And this is the whole thing. You can't empathise with this, not if you haven't lived through it. But there's this need to one-up each other with our own suffering. Well, I'm sorry, some people really do have it worse.

NICOLE
And that's you, is it?

ALICE
Yes, as it happens.

NICOLE *has watched her sister rant with careful calm.*

NICOLE
I think it's time we went back to bed. Is the sofa alright, can you manage?

ALICE
It's fine.

NICOLE
At least let me put away your things. Where did you leave them?

She lifts up the limp cloth bag.

ALICE
This is it.

NICOLE
I thought you said you were staying.

ALICE
I'm not allowed to bring much to the clinic, just a few changes of clothes and some books if they approve them. It's for our own good.

NICOLE
Come on, you can sleep on Mike's side of the bed.

ALICE
He's still gone.

NICOLE
To his mate Dave's, I think. They're probably stealing cars and shooting prostitutes right now. Games, they like video games. That's the first fight we've ever had, I mean a proper one, not about his shoes... He'll come back when he's ready. Or when he runs out of clean pants, whichever's first.

ALICE
And are you ready?

NICOLE
What do you mean?

ALICE
You're getting married, Nic.

NICOLE
It was my idea.

ALICE
That's what I mean. Once we get an idea in our head...

NICOLE
I'm not rushing into things. I weighed up the pros and cons and marrying Mike was the most logical outcome. It's what people do. I'm 27, for God's sake.

ALICE
You're just so different.

NICOLE
We're both lawyers.

ALICE
Don't take it in a bad way. I just always expected you would end up with someone more like... you. Serious and practical and mature.

NICOLE
He can be those things. (*mock-sexy*) You should see him a court of law.

ALICE
Nicole, he calls you 'babe'.

NICOLE
I'm trying to beat that out of him.

ALICE
In a way, it makes perfect sense. You've always wanted someone you could control. He'll be your own personal Pygmalion. I'll help you patch things up. He has to listen to me, I'm sick... I really am sorry about the fight.

Beat.

NICOLE
This has to be the worst Christmas ever.

ALICE
Oh, you forget. Two Christmases ago.

NICOLE
Oh God. Repressed memory surging back. Mum trying to force feed you.

ALICE
In front of everyone.

NICOLE
"Eat this stuffing or I'll stuff it down you!"

ALICE
"You can stuff it!" All I wanted was to take the food to my room.

NICOLE
So you could hide it in the closet. I can still smell the rotting stench when Mum found it days later. The screams. The rats.

ALICE
You see why I was embarrassed. And then she tried to make me eat a Yorkshire pudding. Because "they're mostly air" –

NICOLE
– "they're mostly air –

ALICE
I chewed and chewed on that pudding until it was like wet sand in my mouth, and I started to feel ill but I couldn't leave the table. So I spat.

NICOLE
I'll never forget Nan's face.

ALICE
Like someone died.

Beat.

ALICE
We were trying so hard to act like a normal family having a normal Christmas. I don't know who for.

NICOLE
Do you think Mike will come back?

ALICE
Yeah. And if he doesn't I'll spike his drink with so much lax he'll have no choice but to come back to you for clean pants. He'll shit out his hopes and dreams. You really miss him, don't you?

NICOLE
Oh God. This is horrible. You shouldn't have to see me like this.

ALICE
Like what, in love?

NICOLE
Wanting. Needing. Depending on someone else to make me happy. It's shit. How do people do it? This is rock bottom.

ALICE
Rock bottom? This is your rock bottom?

NICOLE
Yes?

ALICE
I mean, this isn't ideal but I've had a hundred rock bottoms worse than this.

NICOLE
How can you have more than one rock bottom?

ALICE
Easy. You think you've gone as low as you can go, you draw a line under it and say "right, only up from here", I'll never let it get that bad again. But the goalposts have already shifted. The amount of calories you allow yourself gets smaller and smaller. You start weighing yourself every hour and your day is completely ruined if that number moves up even a little bit, even if you know it's just water. You find yourself doing crunches at three in the morning to distract from the hunger pangs that are keeping you awake,

and it's crazy but it's the most natural thing to you to do at three in the morning. You stop brushing your teeth because you're scared there's calories in the toothpaste. You buy cakes only to throw them out, and eat them out of the rubbish bin, half hoping you'll get food poisoning because nothing gets you beach-body-ready like salmonella. You spend 30 pounds on McDonald's and purge it all. Do you know how hard it is to spend 30 pounds at McDonald's? That takes some skill. You trawl the internet for images of sick skeletal women to trigger yourself and hate yourself for it but you can't stop. Stealing food. Stealing pills. Stealing money to buy food and pills. Pissing yourself in public. Shitting yourself in public.

NICOLE
Alright, alright. Jesus, Alice.

ALICE
All I'm saying is, rock bottom has a basement. And even when you think you can't get lower than that, you find out you can survive in the holes in the dirt, in the layers of sediment, and every day you keep falling down, down, down, down.

NICOLE
Was this supposed to make me feel better?

Beat.

ALICE

Shit. Sorry. We always used to know what to say to each other, didn't we? If anyone saw us now, they'd never believe we were sisters.

NICOLE

Don't be stupid. We fight too much to not be related. I'm surprised Mike believed me for a minute.

ALICE

Why did you lie about me?

NICOLE

I didn't lie.

ALICE

I forgot, you omitted the truth. That's so much better.

NICOLE

Do you want me in shackles?

ALICE

I just want to know why.

NICOLE

It wasn't on purpose. God, Alice. I never set out to lie. Of course nobody will believe me now but it's the truth. I'd always been honest about my past. Lying never even occurred to me as an option. I mean, why would it? I hadn't done anything to be ashamed of. It's just that when you're trying to get to know someone for the first time, it's all fun and flirty and then they ask about family and it's like you've swallowed lump of coal, everything is so heavy and hard and bitter. You brush it off and try to change the subject but it's already done. You're not Nicole the lawyer anymore. You're the girl with the dead dad and the sick sister. It's no surprise they never call back, it's one hell of a boner killer. On my first date with Mike he asked about family, and without thinking I started talking about Dad in the present- tense because I'd forgotten for just a moment, you know I still pick up the phone to call him sometimes, and I just caught myself off-guard. "Oh, yeah, my dad's an engineer". And before I could correct myself Mike was talking about his cousins and how he failed his maths GSCEs and I knew I had to fix it but a part of me was so relieved that I didn't have to relive the whole story again and Mike didn't feel sorry for me. He was ripping the piss out of me actually. I said goodbye and went to bed smiling and never thought it would amount to anything. Then he called me. I couldn't believe it. He was so nice and handsome and smart. A bit of a clown but I could work with it. It was never going to last after all. It didn't seem worth it to bring everything down. We were having fun. It was never serious until it was. When we started planning the wedding, that's when I know I should have told him. I had so many chances but... sue me. I didn't want it to change. I didn't want that darkness between us. I knew that as soon as he knew, I wouldn't be his fiancé anymore. I would be a victim. And I couldn't be with someone who pitied me.

Beat.

ALICE
Well.

NICOLE
There, I can't go over it again.

ALICE
That... is total bullshit.

NICOLE
Oh please don't do this, Alice. I believed in you, why can't you believe in me?

ALICE
If you really think that, you must have never believed he loved you in the first place. It's you who has a problem with the past, not everybody else.

NICOLE
Is that your diagnosis?

ALICE
Yes. So don't you dare blame him. The fact is, Mike would have been able to see past it, but for some reason you never could. You just said it now, when you think of me all you see is darkness.

NICOLE
Oh, please.

ALICE
How did you put it – a boner killer.

NICOLE
Must you always be so literal?

ALICE
Do you actually hear yourself? You just said a freaking soliloquy about how you are not your tragedies, while in the same breath reduced my entire existence to my illness. How does that make me feel?

NICOLE
I'm telling you my story. It's not meant to make you feel anything.

ALICE
I'm still here, Nicole. I can still sing badly and make you laugh and give you unwanted hugs. My name is Alice and I love The Great British Bake Off. When I was seven I got kicked out of ballet class for doing the YMCA. I'm really afraid of clowns. I'd like to visit Japan someday. I still, shamefully, have a massive crush on Gary Barlow.

NICOLE
No, Jason was always the hot one.

ALICE
See? We have so many memories, good memories. Don't you miss it? You say so much has changed, but that's just surface stuff. We're twins. We're genetically compatible, for God's sake! We're meant to be together. And if we lived together –

NICOLE
Alice...

ALICE
We could find it again.

NICOLE
Come on.

ALICE
You have no right to say no. This house is half mine.

NICOLE
I just want you think about it. Is it what's best for you? Last time we lived together –

ALICE
I was sick. I forced you into a position you weren't ready for. And I'm sorry. It wasn't fair. But the only reason I'm here now is because I'm ready to recover.

ALICE has taken hold of NICOLE's hands.

NICOLE
Really?

ALICE
And I want your help to continue getting better. Of course you don't have to do anything, but –

NICOLE
Alright.

ALICE
Sorry?

NICOLE
Alright, I will help you. You can stay here.

ALICE *hugs a limp* NICOLE.

ALICE
Thank you, thank you, thank you, thank you.

NICOLE
It's the least I can do.

ALICE
I promise I'll be good.

NICOLE
I can convert our study into a second bedroom. We'll get Mum to send over your stuff.

ALICE
Perfect!

NICOLE
And when business opens up over Christmas I'll help you get your place back at uni.

ALICE
Oh, I –

NICOLE
You *are* going back to university, Alice.

ALICE
Nic.

NICOLE
If we explain your situation, they'll have to take you back. Your doctor can write you a note.

ALICE
A note! I walked out of my final exams, not PE.

NICOLE
Then we threaten legal action. We say it's discrimination. We do one of those articles in the *Daily Mail* crossing our arms and pouting at the camera. Whatever it takes.

ALICE
Can we just slow down a second?

NICOLE
I don't want you sitting around the house all day festering. I'll pay your bills, get everything you need so all you need to do is focus on graduating.

ALICE
I'm just not ready.

NICOLE
You've had three years off! When will you be ready?

ALICE
Yes, three years. I can't just jump back in, I'm rusty.

NICOLE
Come on, you know the ins and outs of the medical system more than anyone.

ALICE
And isn't that exactly the point? Who in their right mind would hire me as a doctor?

NICOLE
You can still practice medicine if you've been sectioned.

ALICE
You've looked into it.

NICOLE
I won't stand by and watch you throw away your talents.

ALICE
My, you flatter me.

NICOLE
You know I'm not one for flattery. The truth is you've always been the smart one. I think we both realised long ago that it was me trying to keep up with you, not the other way around. I'm successful because I work hard. But for you it's always come naturally. It used to turn me green, how can she get by with so little effort when I'm slaving away,

studying night after night? At one time, I admit, I would have been glad to see you wasting your gifts like this. But it's not worth winning if you're not going to put up a fight.

ALICE
I am fighting.

NICOLE
You could have anything you wanted, you know that? Everyone always said it. You're intelligent, kind, prettier than me. All my friends were only friends with me because you're my sister, I just came along with the deal.

ALICE
Please, can you start insulting me again? I'm getting uncomfortable.

NICOLE
I won't stop. Not until you agree to go back to university.

ALICE
Nicole!

NICOLE
Do it. Agree or you can't stay here.

ALICE
I don't think you're in the position to blackmail.

NICOLE
Aren't I? I can call up Mum right this second.

NICOLE *picks up her mobile phone from the counter.*

ALICE
Do it. I'm sure she'd love to hear what you've done with Dad's money.

NICOLE
Right. And then she'll know that I'm the evil sister and she'll never let you stay with me. Either way you're going home.

ALICE
You wouldn't.

NICOLE *types into her phone.*

NICOLE
It's ringing.

ALICE
Alright, alright! I'll apply, that's all. But there's no guaranteed they'll take me back.

NICOLE
They will.

ALICE
I can't believe I just negotiated to live in a house I technically own. I know why you're a lawyer.

NICOLE
Because I always want the best for my client.

ALICE
And now I'd like you to hold up your end of the deal.

NICOLE
I already told you, you can stay here.

ALICE
I want a relationship. I want sleepovers and Netflix nights and bitching about boys. And singing to Take That.

NICOLE
Are we twelve?

ALICE
Come on. Whatever I said, whatever I did, I didn't mean it, I just want you back for good.

NICOLE
It's three in the morning.

ALICE Want you back, want you back –

There is a crunch of gravel and a flash of headlights at the window.

NICOLE
Oh, thank God.

ALICE
Is that...?

NICOLE *runs to the window.*

NICOLE
I knew he'd be back.

She turns to ALICE.

NICOLE
How do I look?

NICOLE *is dishevelled, bleeding, with cake crumbs down her shirt.*

ALICE
Stunning.

The key turns in the lock and MIKE *walks in. He looks somewhat crumpled. He is surprised to see* NICOLE *and* ALICE *standing in the kitchen.*

NICOLE
Mike.

MIKE
Nicole.

NICOLE
How have you been?

MIKE
Since dinner?

NICOLE *laughs. He can barely look at her.*

MIKE
Hello, Alice. Nice to see you haven't scratched each other's eyes out.

ALICE
Just some burns and broken nails.

She points at NICOLE.

MIKE
What happened to you?

NICOLE
It's nothing. An accident.

MIKE
Shame.

NICOLE
I'm glad you're here Mike. I wanted to tell you, Alice is going to be staying with us.

MIKE
With us?

NICOLE
Sure, it may be a bit of a squeeze. But we'll make it work.

ALICE
I won't take up much room.

MIKE
Take as much room as you like. It's your house.

NICOLE
Actually, I'm going to help Alice get back into university.

MIKE (*to* ALICE)
I thought you were taking a break.

NICOLE
She was. But we discussed it and it will be healthy for her to focus on something constructive.

MIKE (*to* ALICE)
Is that what you want?

NICOLE
Of course it is.

MIKE
Alice?

ALICE
I...

MIKE *turns back to* NICOLE, *already knowing the answer.*

MIKE
Look, I'm sorry, Nicole.

NICOLE
It's alright. What matters is you're back now.

MIKE
I thought you'd be asleep. Both of you. I just wanted to get some of my things.

Beat.

NICOLE
Well. You know where the bedroom is.

MIKE *disappears into the bedroom.* NICOLE *and* ALICE *stand stock-still, not saying a word.* MIKE *returns with a game console and some clothes under his arm.*

NICOLE
Clean pants and video games.

MIKE
I'll send for the rest later.

NICOLE
Are you staying with Dave?

MIKE
I'd better be getting back.

NICOLE
Alright.

MIKE *heads for the door.*

NICOLE
For God's sake, Mike. What do you want me to say?

MIKE
Nothing, just nothing.

NICOLE
Should I get on my knees and beg? I fucked up. I'm adult enough to admit it. Now the adult thing to do is forgive me.

MIKE
Forgive you?

NICOLE
You're being really unfair.

MIKE
Me?

NICOLE
So maybe we did rush into things too fast. I can get the money back, we'll sell, whatever. But I only did it to build our future, I did it for you.

MIKE
You really think this is about the money? I mean this really always was the problem with us. You always needed to give something more. A house, a car. Marriage. Acting the perfect girlfriend. Christmas dinner. Well, guess what? You're a shit cook. None of that mattered to me.

NICOLE
Don't lie, Mike. I am not a shit cook.

MIKE
You always needed to justify my love.

NICOLE
I wanted insurance. I wasn't going to invest everything in you and not be sure. I needed to know you weren't going to leave.

MIKE
Why the hell would I leave?

NICOLE
You're leaving now! How long are you going to keep up this grudge? Yes, I made a mistake.

MIKE
It wasn't a mistake though. It was deliberate.

NICOLE
No. Go ask Alice...

MIKE
And what is this now? Calling your first witness to the stand? Are we to give evidence, lay the charges, present our case? How should we settle? At what cost, Nicole?

NICOLE
Mike, calm down.

MIKE

This is one problem you can't argue your way out of. You're a great lawyer. But I didn't fall in love with a lawyer, even though you won't believe it. I fell in love with a person. And it's one thing to lose someone you love, but to find out they never existed –

He begins to cry but won't let her near him. NICOLE *starts to panic.*

NICOLE

Michael. How can you say that? How can you say that?

MIKE

You've killed it.

NICOLE

No, no, no, no. You're getting it all wrong. It was you who let me be who I really am. The real me I was before everything went wrong. Please, Mike. Please. Don't be stupid. Listen to me. Listen to the truth.

MIKE

The thing is, I'll never know now. Whether it is or not. I'll always be wondering if there are more skeletons in your closet. (*to* ALICE) No offence.

ALICE

None taken.

MIKE
You would have been a good sister.

MIKE walks toward the front door.

NICOLE
Mike, what are you doing? Michael!

MIKE
Goodbye, then.

NICOLE
Mike, don't you dare walk away! Don't you dare!

MIKE opens the door and hesitates.

MIKE
Can you promise me something, babe?

NICOLE
Yes, anything, what is it?

MIKE
Get some help.

MIKE exits. NICOLE stands in shock. It's a long, long moment before anyone can speak.

ALICE
Nic, I'm sorry. I'm so sorry.

NICOLE *straightens up, dusts herself off. She turns around, ice-cold and composed like nothing just happened.*

NICOLE
Why?

ALICE
What?

NICOLE
Sorry. I never understood it, when Dad died, people would always apologise. Like they were the ones driving that lorry, like they'd personally glazed the roads in ice that day. *Sorry.*

ALICE
I'm just saying.

NICOLE
But it's different with you, isn't it? Because, out of all people, you have the least to be sorry about. You're the one people should be saying sorry to.

ALICE
I know you're angry.

NICOLE
It almost seems like you say sorry in expectation of an apology. Well, look around. You don't have an audience here.

NICOLE

I mean, you've always had it. This victim complex, ever since you were a kid. Any way you could play the damsel in distress. Running to Dad all the time, sitting on his lap, pretending to cry when you didn't get your way. Getting me in trouble.

ALICE

Oh, did I tattle on you too much? Grow up!

NICOLE *begins to pace.*

NICOLE

It only got worse as you got older. Every week, like clockwork, another crisis of confidence. The never-ending tears, the panic attacks, breaking down so people would have to build you back up. Even when Dad died, you couldn't just grieve like a normal person, you had to get an eating disorder.

ALICE *remains very calm but firm.*

ALICE

I've told you it wasn't about that. This is the problem. How can you understand what it's like to have low self-esteem?

NICOLE *seems affected by this, but straightens up, addressing her sister in a cold, robotic manner.*

NICOLE
I know, we must all hate ourselves. We must all have low self- esteem except let's call it for what it really is – an excuse. An excuse not to perform, an excuse not to try because you might fail. But you know what, the rest of the world just deals with it.

ALICE
You're very cruel.

NICOLE
I am trying to tell you the truth.

ALICE
Oh, you're into truth now, are you?

NICOLE
Do you want to talk about truths? Why are you here, Alice? What could have possibly possessed you to come to me for shelter?

ALICE
We're sisters. I thought that might mean something.

NICOLE
Anything else?

ALICE
Yes. I wanted my money.

NICOLE *turns away.*

NICOLE
I guess it's my turn to confess.

ALICE
What are you talking about?

NICOLE
Do you remember the night Dad died?

ALICE
Bit and pieces. Shrapnel.

NICOLE
Do you remember what you were doing before they told us?

ALICE
No, I...

NICOLE
Think. Just think.

ALICE
We rode in a police car to the hospital. I don't remember crying. It wasn't real.

NICOLE
It was the police who told us. Two of them. They always travel in twos, have you noticed that? Just like in the movies.

ALICE
Yes, I suppose.

NICOLE
They rang the doorbell, stood there on the stoop like they were going to try and sell us a new broadband provider. I thought it must be a cold caller. And I knew. I did. I knew as soon as I saw the two of them standing there wearing their sympathy faces. All I wanted to do was to run to you. I had no idea what I was going to say, I just knew I needed to see your face, I needed to find you... you were in the bathroom. I knew you were in there because I heard you. I heard you in the bathroom. The door was locked and I heard you through the door - I thought you must have heard me through the door, listened all the way down the hall, heard me cry out. How could you not have? And I heard you, I heard you through the locked door, you were throwing up because you heard me scream and that's what people do when they're in shock, they throw up, but when you opened the door, I looked at you and you looked at me and you smiled.

ALICE *is frozen, letting the information wash over her. She's gripping the edge of the counter, dazed and quiet.*

ALICE
What?

NICOLE
Don't make me say it.

ALICE
You knew.

NICOLE
Yes.

ALICE
You knew. But I don't understand. You've known since Dad.

NICOLE
Yes.

ALICE *let's go of the counter and begins to pace up and down, digesting what she has just heard.* NICOLE *exhales as if this secret is a breath she has been holding in all night - for years.*

ALICE
All that time. You carried it on your own.

NICOLE
I'm fine.

ALICE *lets out a spike of laughter.*

ALICE
But you never... Do you know, how often... I kept hoping you'd notice. Maybe today she'll ask me if I'm okay. No. Of course, she doesn't see. It's hard for her. I'm not exactly making it obvious.

NICOLE, *knowing the direction the argument's going, takes the offence.*

NICOLE
You lied to me. You lied to everyone.

ALICE
I was lying to myself.

NICOLE
Oh, give it a rest. Please. Don't insult me. You knew exactly what you were doing. Every time you flushed your dinner down the toilet or wore baggy clothes so no one could see. It was all calculated, Alice.

ALICE
I wasn't trying to manipulate you. It does whatever it can to survive.

NICOLE
Yes, "Ana" made you do it. "Ana" made you starve yourself. "Mia" made you throw it all back up. Together they conspired and blackmailed you, they held a gun to your head until you had to lie to everyone and hide food and steal –

ALICE
You're one to talk.

NICOLE
You're looking for anyone to blame but yourself.

ALICE

You're loving this, aren't you? Now this is the part I don't understand. God knows you love nothing more than to call me out on my shit. But you heard every single lie I spewed out and you didn't say a word. You just let me convince everyone it was grief.

NICOLE

I knew you'd find a way to make this my fault. You chose to deceive everyone. You chose to lie.

Now ALICE *has frozen in her steps, growing sick with realisation.*

ALICE

No, but it's not just about holding me accountable, is it? You knew I was sick. All that time we were living together. You... oh, God... you watched. For months. I got sicker and smaller. Didn't you wonder what was going to happen to me? Weren't you scared?

NICOLE

It's not my responsibility.

ALICE

It was our neighbour who sent for help. I didn't even know her, she was just coming over to complain about the bins and she took one look at me. You'd gone out shopping.

NICOLE

I was buying groceries, someone has to do it.

ALICE
How much longer would you have waited?

NICOLE
And if I'd told you to stop, you would have, I suppose. What exactly did you want me to do?

ALICE
I wanted you to try!

ALICE has screamed this, but NICOLE keeps her cool. She takes a step towards her sister, seeming to want to make peace.

NICOLE
Okay. Okay. From now on, I will try to help you. I will take you to doctors you won't listen to. I will prepare you special meals you won't eat. I will buy you prescription medication and take you to get your stomach pumped when you overdose. I will hide knives in odd places that you will find again and again. I will put my entire life on hold and pour every bit of energy into "helping" you, and you'll HATE me in return.

NICOLE grabs a fist-full of Christmas cake off the counter and smothers it onto ALICE's mouth, using her other arm to get her in a stranglehold. ALICE screams with a closed mouth, trying to wriggle away.

NICOLE
You want my help? This is how I'm helping you. This is how I'm helping you. Go on. Take it. Help yourself. Stop killing yourself. Stop killing yourself. Stop killing yourself. Why are you killing yourself?

ALICE *breaks free. She gasps, wiping every free every trace of food.*

ALICE
I hate you.

NICOLE
But this is what you wanted, right? Somebody to call the shots for you. Don't you think it's time we admitted what this is all about. Your goddamn fear of responsibility.

ALICE
Oh, fuck off.

NICOLE
No, you listen. Think back to when all of this started. It was our last year at university, remember. Life was about to start, finally. Careers, proper boyfriends. And then we decided to move out of home and that's when you snapped. That was it. Suddenly you realised you had to be an adult and it freaked you the fuck out. You couldn't handle it. You might have to make some decisions on your own and you'd be the only person to blame if it all went tits up. So you decided not to try. You wanted everyone else to look after you so you wouldn't have to. You wanted to get rid

of anything that made you a woman. You starved yourself until you were a little girl again.

ALICE *is pale, still as silence. When she speaks, she is very quiet.*

ALICE
Oh, my God.

NICOLE
You know that it's true, don't you?

ALICE
I can't believe it.

NICOLE
Well, now you know.

ALICE
Fuck. You really are that ignorant.

NICOLE
I don't think –

ALICE
Then you shouldn't talk.

NICOLE
Alice, be honest with yourself for once in your life.

ALICE
I am. I thought I wanted your help but I realise now. There's no way in hell you could help me.

NICOLE
I think you knew that.

ALICE
What?

NICOLE
Why are you here? Why are you here, Alice? Why did you come to me? Why didn't you go to Mum's?

ALICE
Alright, you've already made it pretty clear I'm not wanted.

ALICE starts packing up her things.

NICOLE
Why don't you want Mum to visit you anymore? Why won't you let me call her?

ALICE
Why do you care?

NICOLE
What about Mum makes you so uncomfortable?

ALICE
I'm not talking anymore.

NICOLE
See, you've already lived with me. You know I'll let you do whatever you want, you're an adult, you can fuck up your own life, I don't have the time for it. But Mum's heart breaks. She doesn't give in. She'll cry and beg you eat until you can't take it anymore. That Christmas, I saw Mum. It was midnight and she was standing in the kitchen washing jars in soapy water so you couldn't read the labels. That's why you came to me. All this earnestness, the way you go around proclaiming the evils of magazines. You give yourself very good advice, you just rarely follow it. Well, here's some advice. Stop pretending. You don't want to recover at all.

ALICE *drops her belongings.*

NICOLE
Alice?

ALICE
You're right.

Silence.

ALICE
What am I doing? How am I a stranger to myself? I thought things would be different by now. If I lost the weight everything would fall into place. I'd be different. Happy. The

awkward ugly bits of me would come together. But it didn't work. I wasn't good enough. And now I have nothing. And I don't want it. I don't want to want it anymore.

ALICE starts to sob.

NICOLE
I guess denial runs in the family.

Beat.

NICOLE
That night I found out about you. I couldn't process it, not when Dad had just... And then, when everyone else started to notice, they guessed it was the grief. Isn't it normal to lose your appetite? I started to hold on to that, even though I knew it wasn't true, deep down, but it's funny, you can convince yourself of almost anything if you really try.

She's tearful despite her best efforts to control it.

NICOLE
You want to say I disappeared. You disappeared before my very eyes. You let this thing take you when I needed you most. I needed somebody to talk to, I needed a shoulder to cry on. And instead, I had to worry about you. I had to check on you in the bath to make you hadn't drowned because you were too weak to lift your head. At the funeral nobody asked if I was okay because you fainted during the procession. You never asked...

ALICE cries harder.

ALICE
I'm sorry.

NICOLE
No, stop. Don't do that. You always do this. Your emotions are so big there's no room for anybody else. You would drown in your own tears if you could. It's not fair. You force me to be this way. Why is it always you who gets to feel? Don't you think it would be easier for me to break too? I'm so tired of being strong.

She's now sobbing, ALICE *watching in shock.*

NICOLE
*Please s*top making me. I can't do it, I can't do it anymore. You hear me? Dad died, Alice. What you're doing is so much worse. Because you have a choice. You're letting go. And I can't be alone again.

ALICE *is very still and silent.*

ALICE
You're not alone. I'm here. And you're right. I should have been there for you. I hope you can forgive me.

NICOLE
I think we're just two people who've had a shit time.

ALICE
Yes.

A long pause. ALICE *picks up her bag again.*

NICOLE
What are you doing?

ALICE
Getting my stuff.

NICOLE
I can see that, but why?

ALICE
I think it's time for me to leave.

NICOLE
What are you talking about? I told you, you could stay here.

ALICE
I know and you've been very generous.

NICOLE
Alice, don't start this now.

ALICE
Start what?

NICOLE
Whatever it is you're trying to do. We're both in pain.

ALICE *stops for a moment.*

ALICE
You're right. We have both been in a lot of pain. But through it all, I kept wondering why, the person who hurt me the most was you.

NICOLE
I didn't mean to hurt you, Alice.

ALICE
Now who isn't taking responsibility?

NICOLE
I never wanted to hurt you.

ALICE
Maybe you didn't. I think that's the problem. I think you trigger me. I think that's why I wanted to come here. In the back of my mind, that's what I wanted.

NICOLE
No, no, Alice.

ALICE
Thank you. I didn't know that until you showed me. And now I have to go.

NICOLE
Alice, you can't go out there in your nightie, for God's sake. You'll catch your death.

ALICE
Can I borrow some clothes?

NICOLE
Nothing will fit.

ALICE
I'll get creative.

NICOLE
Alice.

ALICE
I'll find some myself then.

ALICE *disappears out the door leading to the rest of the house.* NICOLE *paces up and down. A long moment passes.* ALICE *reappears in a black blouse, black slacks, pumps and a black coat.*

NICOLE
Alice.

ALICE
I hope you don't mind me borrowing your coat, I got sick on mine.

NICOLE
Keep it. You look beautiful.

ALICE
Can I borrow your car? I'll get it back to you, somehow.

NICOLE
It's four in the morning, Alice.

ALICE
Nicole. Car keys.

NICOLE
No.

ALICE *sees them hanging on a hook by the front door and takes them.*

NICOLE
I'll have you arrested. Grand theft auto.

ALICE
Now that would be something.

She turns to the front door.

NICOLE
Anything you need. I'll do it. I'll help you get better.

ALICE
Do you really believe that?

NICOLE
Well, fuck you, then. Save me.

ALICE
I'm sorry.

ALICE *starts to walk away.*

NICOLE
Wait! Just wait one second. Please. Wait.

NICOLE *goes to the counter. She pulls out a large Tupperware container. Then she fills it with various Christmas foods from the fridge. She runs back to* ALICE *and gives it to her.*

NICOLE
For the road.

ALICE *takes the food.*

NICOLE
Don't leave me.

ALICE *wraps her arms around* NICOLE. *For once,* NICOLE *returns the hug.* ALICE *lets go.*

ALICE
I promise, when I come back, you'll be able to hug me without flinching.

ALICE *exits through the door. Surely, we hear the crunch of gravel on the driveway, see the headlights in the windows.* NICOLE *enters her dark house, weeping silently. She is once again alone.*

--------------------------- *END* ---------------------------

I and the Village

by Darren Donohue

I and the Village follows three African women living in the Direct Provision system. Direct Provision is the system asylum seekers must enter while awaiting a decision on their applications in Ireland. Regrettably, many asylum seekers live in the system for years, and *I and the Village* looks at the dire consequences of this long-term confinement.

Cast & Creatives

I and the Village by Darren Donohue was first performed at The Bread & Roses Theatre from 25th May to 5th June 2021, with the following cast and creatives:

<u>Cast:</u>

JETA
Chido Kunene

KEICHA
Funke Adeleke

HANNAH
Laide Sonola

CARL
Mark Rush

Creatives:

Directors
Velenzia Spearpoint & Rebecca Pryle

Researcher & Dramaturg
Matilda Velevitch

Assistant Director
Tom Ward

Producer
Natalie Chan

Set & Costume Designer
Constance Villemot

Sound & Lighting Designer
Chuma Emembolu

Stage Manager
Olivia Pryle

Technical Operator
Daniel Foggo

Creative Producer
Tessa Hart

Assistant Producer
Daniel Cartlidge

Rehearsal Photography
Jake Owens

Finance & Funding Manager
Lynne McConway

Offies 2021 Nomination for: Performance Ensemble.

Characters

KEICHA is from Nigeria and is 38 years old. She can appear vulnerable and unsure but is also fiercely determined and strong-willed. Keicha is living in the Direct Provision System for 8 years.

JETA is from Zimbabwe and is 36 years old. She's intelligent and articulate, she's also highly intuitive and compassionate. Jeta is living in the Direct Provision System for 6 years.

HANNAH is from Nigeria and is 18 years old. She's quick tempered, extremely sharp-witted and streetwise. Hannah has just entered the Direct Provision System.

CARL is from Millstreet, Co. Cork and is 38 years old. He's friendly and good-natured, possessing a lively sense of humour. Carl is Centre Manager at the Direct Provision Centre.

Setting

Story outline

Keicha and Jeta have shared a room for years, their memories and fantasies merging into one story of longing and survival. When eighteen-year-old Hannah arrives, she finds herself swept up in their reality and must fight to maintain her sense of identity.

Set

The action takes place in Drishane Castle, Direct Provision Centre, Co. Cork. Our set is the room Keicha, Jeta and Hannah share in the Direct Provision Centre. There are three beds, one – stage left (*Hannah's bed*), one – stage right (*Jeta's bed*), one – centre stage (*Keicha's bed*). There is a small locker beside each bed and an old-fashioned portable TV sits on Keicha's locker.

Time

The present.

Scenes
All these scenes take place in the room.

Scene 1	Keicha and Carl.
Scene 2	Keicha and Jeta.
Scene 3	Jeta and Hannah.
Scene 4	Jeta and Carl.
Scene 5	Hannah, Keicha and Jeta.
Scene 6	Hannah, Carl, Keicha and Jeta.

Note
/ indicates a sudden interruption or interjection.
! indicates a heightened delivery of dialogue (not shouting).

Scene 1

Morning. In gloomy darkness, Carl attempts to screw a lightbulb into the bedside lamp. It flickers on and off as Keicha stands watching.

CARL (*Frustrated, struggling with the lightbulb*)
Yeah, it's stubborn all right. Go on, get in. Nearly there... go on. I swear to god! Get in, you... you little beggar!

KEICHA (*Flat*)
Maybe if you speak nicely to the bulb it'll cooperate.

Carl shoots Keicha a quick look and returns to the chore.

CARL (*Smiles*)
Lovely little bulb, the best little bulb in Ireland, sit in the socket for me? Got ya!

KEICHA
You see? It only needed a little sweet talk.

Carl gives the bulb an extra twist and triumphantly tests it.

CARL (*Delighted*)
Good now. On we go, where we stop nobody knows.

Lights come up on stage as Carl moves to the second lamp and changes the bulb.

CARL
Strange... they went together.

KEICHA
What?

CARL
It's strange all the bulbs blew at the same time.

KEICHA
We were having a party.

CARL
A party?

KEICHA
Jumping around and flashing the lights. That's what we do all night.

CARL (*Smiles*)
I often wondered what you got up to.

KEICHA (*Playful*)
Down behind reception, fingering your big bunch of keys?

CARL
What's that?

KEICHA
You, fingering your big bunch of keys and thinking about Jeta.

CARL
Jeta?

KEICHA
And me jumping around our little palace.

Carl changes the final bulb and it blinks on.

CARL
Now... I've brought the light back into your lives.

Carl lifts a battered suitcase onto Hannah's bed and places a booklet on it.

CARL
I'll leave it here and please, make sure she gets this (*booklet*). I'm not about later and Tony has a head like a sieve.

KEICHA
Is she Syrian?

CARL
No... no, she's African.

KEICHA
Good, we don't want those Syrians coming over here and stealing our beds.

CARL (*Smiles*)
No... she could be your long lost neighbour she's Nigerian.

KEICHA
My neighbour? How many people live in Nigeria?

CARL (*Playful*)
Is there anyone left over there?

KEICHA
160 million.

CARL
Sounds overcrowded, you must love all these big green fields.

KEICHA (*Stern*)
We don't come here for the scenery.

CARL No?

KEICHA
We come here for the weather.

Carl laughs.

KEICHA
So, it's unlikely she's my long lost neighbour.

CARL
You never know it's a small world, isn't that what they say?

KEICHA
Who says that?

CARL
People.

KEICHA
People living on a *small* island in a *big* world.

CARL
Once met a first cousin of mine in Time Square, New York. Bumped into Martin out of the blue, nearly knocked him over, you couldn't make it up. We've an old saying, you can go nowhere without your backdoor.

KEICHA (*Unimpressed*)
We also have a saying, show the moon to a child and it sees only your finger.

CARL
What does that mean?

KEICHA
Ask our new arrival when she gets here. Judging by her suitcase she has the answer.

CARL (*Serious*)
I hear she'd a rough time of it all right. Been through a few foster homes, in and out of emergency accommodation.

KEICHA
How old is she?

CARL
Just turned eighteen.

KEICHA
Where are her parents?

CARL
Who knows, they're not here anyways. The girl's fending for herself, has been since she arrived.

KEICHA
What time does she get in?

CARL
Late tomorrow. (*Indicating the booklet*) You might go through it with her, show her the ropes?

KEICHA
We'll put the champagne on ice and roll out a red carpet.

CARL
I appreciate that. Anything else while I'm here?

KEICHA
We need traps.

CARL
Mousetraps?

KEICHA (*Nods*)
They're moving in from the fields. This weather makes them bolder, they forget their fear.

CARL (*Sighs*)
It's impossible to keep them out of these old buildings.

KEICHA
Kenede's little boy spotted a rat in their bedroom.

CARL
A rat?

KEICHA
He was playing his mouthorgan and saw it shoot across the floor. Without thinking, he threw the mouthorgan and stunned it. Kenede found him petting it like the rat was a new puppy.

CARL
Jaysus...

KEICHA
Before she could slap him the rat jumped up and shot out the door. I hear them scratching under the floorboards, they're moving in from the fields.

CARL
Don't worry, leave it with me. If we have to we'll get someone in - an exterminator.

KEICHA
And the traps?

CARL
I'll pop into the village after lunch. I've to go in for something anyway.

KEICHA
All right.

CARL
Anything else?

Keicha shakes her head.

CARL
The room's chilly. I'll bleed those radiators at the weekend, it'll make a big difference. Remind me and I'll take care of it. Right, no rest for the wicked. I'll see you later.

Carl moves to leave.

KEICHA
Don't run off.

CARL
I've to open the kitchen, Keicha.

KEICHA (*Playful*)
First give me your autograph.

CARL
My autograph?

KEICHA
Didn't I see your little face on a poster by the bus stop?

CARL (*Penny drops*)
Ah...

KEICHA
Ah *yes*! You're an actor.

CARL
A chancer.

KEICHA
You're in a play.

CARL
I am, god help me.

KEICHA
What is it?

CARL
A bit of a comedy, priests and pushy housekeepers.

KEICHA
Sounds fun.

CARL
Well, half the lads won't learn their lines leaving the rest of us nervous wrecks.

KEICHA
That's unprofessional.

CARL
Well, we're not professionals, we're amateurs - chancers. But the locals get a laugh out of it and I suppose that's the main thing.

KEICHA
What do you do in the play?

CARL
Make an eejit of myself.

KEICHA
I'd like to see that.

CARL (*Smiles*)
Don't you see it every day?

KEICHA
I'd like to see it *on stage*.

Carl laughs.

KEICHA
When I was a little girl I'd make up my own plays.

CARL
Oh yeah?

KEICHA
I'd make up the stories and assign everyone their roles.

CARL
They all jumped when you barked?

KEICHA
They'd no choice, I was the boss.

CARL
I well believe it!

KEICHA
We performed them in a clearing outside our village. Our mothers worked hard, turning Cassava roots into gari for big hotels. They'd scold us for wasting our time playacting.

CARL
What're Cassava roots?

KEICHA
They're like our potatoes.

CARL
Really?

KEICHA
You peel and grate them into a mash, then you roast it.

CARL
What's it taste like?

KEICHA
Chicken.

Carl laughs.

KEICHA
You'd have to try it for yourself.

CARL
Sounds like a lot of work?

KEICHA
It was but once their lunchbreak came they'd run out to see us. Behind all their protests they loved it – our songs, the dancing – they'd join in and take over.

CARL
Sounds like my mother and Aunts.

KEICHA
Our final performance was the story of Ituen and the King's Wife. Do you know it?

CARL
I don't think so.

KEICHA (*Smiles*)
Ituen is caught having an affair with the King's wife.

CARL
I'm guessing that's not good?

KEICHA
King Offiong tells his men to take Ituen into the bush and deal with him according to native custom. The men tie Ituen to a tree, then with a sharp knife they cut off his jaw and carry it back to the King. Of course, I was playing Ituen, I always gave myself the best roles.

Carl laughs.

KEICHA
I was tied to the tree with a red bandage around my chin. But at the end, instead of our mothers laughing and patting our heads, there was silence. I looked up to see what was wrong and my mother had turned her face away, she couldn't look at me. I suppose she knew about the

trouble brewing in our district. (*Sighs*) That was our final performance, not long after it wasn't safe to go out.

CARL (*Awkward*)
Trouble in paradise?

KEICHA
That's one way to put it.

Beat.

CARL (*Anxious*)
Is Jeta about?

KEICHA
She's gone to the village.

CARL
Right.

KEICHA (*Teasing*)
Do you miss her?

CARL
No... no, I was going to say it later, after lunch/

KEICHA
Say *what*?

CARL
I wanted to... well, I wanted to talk about the curfews. But we can do it later, Keicha, after lunch in the office if you prefer?

KEICHA (*Sharp*)
You're here now if something's caught in your throat, spit it out.

Keicha moves to the booklet, picks it up and flicks through it.

CARL (*Hesitant*)
Well, you need to let us know when you're planning to stay away overnight. You know that, Keicha.

KEICHA (*Reading from the booklet*)
If you plan to be away from the centre overnight, you must let the Centre Manager know in advance.

CARL
Yes... it's for your own safety. We need to know you're all right, that something hasn't happened.

KEICHA (*Reading*)
The Centre Manager is obliged to notify the Community Welfare Officer if you've been away without telling management.

CARL
Don't worry about that, I only want to have a chat/

KEICHA (*Reading*)
This may affect your entitlement to collect Direct Provision Allowance/

CARL
That's not going to happen. Just remember in future to let us know/

KEICHA (*Reading*)
You must not seek employment. You must not cook in your room or store food. You must not consume alcohol or create excessive noise. You must not *redecorate* your room. (*Laughs, looking about*) RE decorate!

CARL
Keicha/

KEICHA (*Closing the booklet*)
It's hard to remember everything.

CARL (*Firm*)
Well, I'm asking you to remember *this*. You need to let us know/

KEICHA (*Flippant*)
You're the angry father, I'm the naughty child.

CARL
It's not just for me. Jeta was worried sick.

KEICHA
Jeta again? It all comes back to Jeta for you.

CARL
What?

Keicha sits on the bed beside the suitcase.

CARL
Right well, I said my bit and we'll leave it at that. We'll say no more about it.

KEICHA
Don't you want to know where I went?

CARL
Well... if you want to tell me.

KEICHA
I was with friends at a birthday party with lots of people. There was food and... and music. Everyone was excited to see me, they appreciated the effort I made to get there.

CARL
Good, that's good. Where was it?

KEICHA
Cork city, a lovely ballroom in a beautiful hotel. They put me up, my friends, they paid for the hotel room.

CARL
It sounds like a good night?

KEICHA
I felt like a princess.

CARL
Well, that's good. I know it's difficult being cooped up here/

KEICHA (*Snaps*)
Difficult?

CARL
I mean, I'm glad you'd a good night, Keicha. I didn't mean to stick my nose in. I was just worried is all.

KEICHA
You're worried about *me*?

CARL
Well, not just you. I don't want you thinking you're being singled out or anything. It's my job to look out for everyone here.

KEICHA (*Cutting*)
You've a big heart.

CARL (*Uneasy*)
Right, I'll give you a shout when I get back with the traps. If you need anything else, you know where I am. I'll... I'll see you later.

Keicha nods and Carl exits. Keicha stands, opens the suitcase and places her hand on the lid.

Scene 2

Evening. The lights subtly change suggesting evening and there's a sound of people, indistinguishable voices and traffic. Eventually the sounds fade and Jeta enters carrying a Spar shopping bag.

KEICHA
Where were you?

JETA (*Tired*)
Fucking Spar.

KEICHA
What took so long?

JETA
Leave me alone, I'm tired.

Jeta moves to her bed and sits.

KEICHA
I thought something happened.

JETA
Nothing happened.

KEICHA
So, what kept you?

JETA
There was a queue.

KEICHA
A queue?

JETA
A big queue in fucking Spar. An old woman carrying a little dog held everyone up, she kept talking about the weather and feeding the dog chocolate. The dog wore a little overcoat covered in fake diamonds. (*Bitter*) When she finished, when she pushed by me to the door, I told her.

KEICHA
Told her *what*?

Jeta doesn't respond

KEICHA (*Stern*)
What did you say?

JETA (*Angry*)
All right...

Jeta stands and recreates the geography of Spar.

JETA
Here are the aisles, all the rows of shit. There's the Lotto machine, farting out tickets. There's the crisp packets all different colours. You stand here.

KEICHA
Where?

JETA
By the counter holding the dog.

KEICHA
What dog?

Jeta takes a toilet roll from the Spar bag and crams it under Keicha's arm.

JETA
Now. Feed him a chocolate. (*Jeta points to the toilet roll*) Push a chocolate into its fat mouth.

Keicha mimes feeding the toilet roll a chocolate.

JETA (*Smiles*)
The mutt gave a big woof.

Jeta waits expectantly and Keicha gives a little woof.

JETA
Good. Now, push by me.

KEICHA
Push by you?

JETA
To the door.

Keicha hesitates.

JETA
You want to know what I said?

Keicha walks by Jeta, moving to the door. But when she reaches Jeta, Jeta roughly takes hold of Keicha's arm.

JETA (*Reprimanding*)
She didn't walk like that. Do it again. Pin back your shoulders, stick out your arse.

Keicha retreats, composes herself and walks toward Jeta, walking upright, her head in the air. Jeta roughly grabs her arm and points to the toilet roll.

JETA (*Intense*)
When people start dressing their dogs, the dogs start making plans.

KEICHA
That's what you said?

JETA
Now, call me a black whore.

KEICHA
She didn't say that.

JETA
She was thinking it. They all were.

Jeta releases Keicha, sits on her bed and digs through the shopping bag.

JETA
Want to know how much money I've left?

KEICHA
What did you buy?

JETA
Not a penny, I spent every last penny. Of course, €19.10 doesn't stretch far, not in a fine establishment like fucking Spar.

KEICHA
What did you buy?

JETA
I wanted to buy cigarettes but when I handed over the money (*With scorn*) *The Manageress* said, I hadn't enough. They'd shot up 40 cent in the budget, gone out of my price bracket. Had to scoop up my pennies, rethink my shopping list.

Jeta dips into the Spar bag and produces a packet of buns. She rips them open and chooses one.

KEICHA (*Annoyed*)
What're you doing?

JETA
Eating a bun. Want one?

KEICHA
If you're caught, you'll be punished.

JETA
Leave me alone, I'm hungry. Here, take one.

Keicha shakes her head and Jeta takes a big bite.

KEICHA (*Stern*)
You're spilling crumbs, they invite rats.

JETA
They're welcome to the place.

KEICHA
They carry disease, infect everything they touch.

JETA (*Pointed*)
It's rats on two legs *you* should worry about.

KEICHA
What?

JETA
I met Ray.

KEICHA
Where?

JETA
Signing out, he was signing in.

KEICHA
What did he want?

JETA
To speak with you. He wants to speak with you in his room. He said to call by later.

KEICHA
What time?

JETA (*Suspicious*)
All he said was *you'd* know what it was about.

KEICHA
I don't.

JETA
So he was mistaken?

KEICHA
Yes.

JETA
He's a man of the street.

KEICHA
I know that.

JETA
Did you borrow money?

KEICHA
No.

JETA
I could help you.

KEICHA
Help me?

JETA
Pay him back.

KEICHA
I didn't borrow money.

JETA
He's a man of the street, everything he touches shatters into a million pieces/

KEICHA (*Strong, changing the subject*)
Get me a glass of water.

JETA
What?

KEICHA
I'm thirsty.

JETA
You're thirsty?

KEICHA (*Commanding*)
Get me a glass of water.

Jeta stands, retrieves a water bottle and brings it to Keicha.

KEICHA
What's this?

JETA
Water.

KEICHA (*Sharp*)
I won't drink out of that. Pour the water into a glass.

Jeta moves away, finding a glass. Keicha moves to the open suitcase and looks down on it. Jeta brings her a glass of water.

KEICHA
Put it on my locker.

Jeta hobbles over to Keicha's bedside locker.

KEICHA
You're limping?

JETA
I need new shoes, these shoes are worn out. Asked Carl for my clothing allowance, I asked him for the form. (*Proud*) Told him, when I worked at the university I'd many pairs of shoes. I told him all about it. He smiled, I think he understood. Wrote it down in a file, my request/

KEICHA
He's married.

JETA
Who's married?

KEICHA
Carl.

JETA
So what?

KEICHA
He has a wife.

JETA
He wears no wedding band.

KEICHA
Her name is Helen. They've two children, a house in Cork overlooking the church.

JETA
How do you know?

KEICHA
I asked him. Last summer they went to Euro Disney, they simply booked the tickets and jumped on a plane. He showed me a picture on his phone. His wife is blond with blue eyes, very pretty. The boy is fair just like his mother, the little girl is dark like Carl/

JETA (*Defiant*)
He wears no wedding band.

KEICHA
Some men don't.

JETA
Why did you ask him?

KEICHA
What?

JETA
About his family?

KEICHA
We got talking.

JETA
When?

KEICHA (*Laughs*)
When? I don't know – last week, the week before.

JETA
Did you talk about me?

KEICHA
You?

JETA
What did you say?

KEICHA
Nothing.

JETA
What did you tell him?

KEICHA
We didn't talk about you.

JETA (*Hurt*)
You didn't?

KEICHA
We talked about his home, his wife, the holiday with his children/

JETA
He never mentioned a family.

KEICHA
Did you ever ask him?

JETA (*Angry*)
Why should I? It's none of my business! What do I care if he has ten wives!

KEICHA
He dropped off a case. Said, to expect a new arrival.

Keicha digs around in the suitcase.

KEICHA
I said, we'd roll out the red carpet, have our little palace sparkling like a diamond.

Keicha plucks an old fashioned alarm clock from the case.

KEICHA
What time is it?

Jeta doesn't respond. Keicha winds the alarm clock and places it back. She digs around again, finds a dress and pulls it from the suitcase.

KEICHA
Here, put this on.

JETA
Why?

KEICHA
To see if it fits.

Jeta moves to Keicha and takes the dress. She lays it out on the bed, undresses and stands uncertainly.

KEICHA What're you waiting for?

Jeta puts on the dress. Keicha finds a small jewellery box and lifts it from the suitcase. She opens it and investigates the contents.

JETA (*Pulling at the dress*)
It's too tight.

KEICHA
It's perfect.

JETA
It pinches.

KEICHA
It's perfect. Sit here.

Through this section Jeta sits on the bed, Keicha places a necklace around her neck and fastens the clasp. She also clips on earrings, places bracelets on her wrists and ties Jeta's hair back.

KEICHA
When I was a little girl my mother would dress me up. After a hot bath she'd dress me up like I was her doll. She put me in my Sunday clothes and I'd model them for her. I was the youngest, her pet. If I did well and pleased her, she'd reward me, promise me something I wanted. She'd dress me up when I was a child and now, I'll do the same with you. Stand up.

JETA
I don't want to.

Keicha moves to stand before Jeta.

KEICHA
Get up.

JETA
No.

Keicha takes hold of Jeta's chin and lifts her. Jeta stands, Keicha moves to her bedside locker and drinks some water.

KEICHA
One evening, two men came. They wore uniforms. One was silent, watching me. The other turned the place upside-down. When he finished, he said, you've five minutes to gather your things. My mother pleaded with him. Told him, we'd nowhere to go. He said, you're coming with us. (*To Jeta*) Walk toward the door.

Jeta hesitates but moves toward the door. The pace increases through this section.

KEICHA (*Sharp*)
Where're you going?

JETA
Nowhere.

KEICHA
You're going out.

JETA
No.

KEICHA
It's not safe, there's trouble on the street.

JETA
I'm not going anywhere.

KEICHA
You're all dressed up, you're meeting someone.

JETA
No/

KEICHA
You think there's nothing to fear. I protected you well, kept you sheltered, safe. You think someone is waiting for you?

JETA
I don't/

KEICHA
His name is Farinose. I've seen you together. Show me how you walk for him. Show me how you'll walk *to* him.

Jeta moves to Keicha.

KEICHA
Where are you now?

JETA
I don't know.

KEICHA
You went out.

JETA
Yes.

KEICHA
You disobeyed me.

JETA
Yes.

KEICHA
He didn't come.

JETA
No.

KEICHA
It's night.

JETA
They're breaking all the windows, looting the shops. Someone's lying in the street.

KEICHA (*Animated*)
Yes.

JETA
Very still, holding a radio. I hear the music, recognise the song. Someone pushes me over.

KEICHA
Run home.

JETA
I crawl through the broken glass. Trucks fly by full of soldiers pointing guns, taking aim/

KEICHA
Run home!

JETA
Someone takes my hand, he lifts me to my feet.

KEICHA
He?

JETA
Came.

KEICHA
Who?

JETA (*Triumphant*)
Farinose!

KEICHA
No…

JETA
He's smiling, he's not afraid! He's holding flowers!

KEICHA (*Angry*)
No!

JETA (*Defiant*)
I was mistaken! The fires are fireworks, the trucks are floats full of people! Everyone waves flags, everyone cheers! The boy with the radio is dancing and pulling my sleeve!

KEICHA (*Sharp*)
Stop it!

JETA
It's James, my little brother! He pulls me into the street and Farinose dresses me in flowers! Everyone moves around us! Farinose takes hold of me!

Jeta aggressively takes hold of Keicha's hands.

JETA
We spin faster and faster! Everything spinning around us!

Jeta begins spinning with Keicha pulling her around in a circle.

JETA
Nothing can touch us! No one can harm us!

Keicha roughly pulls away from Jeta, she moves downstage and looks out. Jeta continues to spin faster.

JETA (*Euphoric*)
We're swept forward and placed on thrones! We're King and Queen of the carnival!

Jeta collapses on her bed and buries her face in a pillow.

JETA
Everyone falls silent. They're waiting for us to kiss.

Jeta holds the pillow as though it were Farinose.

JETA (*Playful*)
Well, how about it, Farinose? We don't want to disappoint them.

Jeta turns the pillow away from her.

JETA (*To Keicha*)
Now, he's shy. (*To pillow*) Farinose, don't be shy. Give your Jeta a little kiss, let me feel your feathery lips. (*Seductive*) Touch me, Farinose. Touch me... *touch me...*

Keicha moves swiftly to Jeta, snatches the pillow out of her grasp and hits her over the head with it.

JETA (*Defiant*)
Oh Farinose! Such a kiss! My head is spinning! Kiss me again!

KEICHA (*Furious*)
There's no kiss! No celebration! There's nothing!

JETA (*Cruel*)
Is that what you said in their office, sipping their tea and blowing your nose?

KEICHA (*Strong*)
Take off the dress.

JETA
Why?

KEICHA
Put it back in the case.

JETA
I think I'll keep it.

KEICHA
Put the jewellery back in its box. Leave everything as it was.

Keicha moves toward the door.

JETA
Where you going?

KEICHA
Out.

JETA
Where?

KEICHA
To the canteen.

JETA
What for?

KEICHA
I'm hungry.

JETA
It's too early.

KEICHA
I know that.

JETA
The canteen is closed.

KEICHA
I'm going to wait.

JETA
Outside?

KEICHA
Yes.

JETA
It's going to snow.

Keicha moves toward the door and Jeta stands.

JETA
I'll come with you.

KEICHA
No.

JETA
Why not?

They consider each other intently for a moment before Keicha moves to her bed and lies down.

JETA
Are you going to sleep?

Keicha doesn't answer.

JETA
Will I turn on the TV?

Keicha doesn't respond and Jeta moves to the TV.

KEICHA
I'm not going to sleep.

JETA
You're resting?

KEICHA
I'm thinking.

JETA
What about?

Keicha doesn't respond and Jeta moves to sit by her.

JETA (*Tentative*)
Keicha? Are you angry with me?

Keicha doesn't respond.

JETA
We need more blankets. I'll speak to Carl. We can curl up beneath them and I'll keep you warm. Are you asleep?

KEICHA
Yes.

JETA (*Playful*)
What time is it over there?

KEICHA
Morning.

JETA
What kind of day is it?

KEICHA
Beautiful.

JETA
Tell me.

KEICHA
The sun is up. The morning mist is fading.

JETA
And the village?

Beat.

JETA
And the village? Keicha?

KEICHA
Tuesday...

JETA
Tuesday?

KEICHA
Or the day before... I met a man.

JETA
What man?

KEICHA
A man in a big white van.

JETA
Where?

KEICHA
On the road.

JETA
What did he want?

KEICHA
To look up my skirt. Told him, there's nothing to see. He asked me to prove it. So... so I did.

JETA
On the road?

KEICHA
By a ditch. He leaned out the window holding up his phone. He didn't look at me, he never took his eyes from the screen. I held my bag between my teeth.

JETA
Why?

KEICHA
So... I could raise my skirt. His phone rang and he jumped like he'd been pinched. He spoke awhile, told someone he was running late. Then he spat at me and... and drove off.

JETA (*Disturbed*)
But why would you do that? It's dangerous! He could've hurt you, thrown you in the back of his van.

KEICHA I'm sorry.

JETA
What good is being *sorry*? You can't do that.

KEICHA
I'm sorry.

JETA (*Strong*)
Don't do it again.

KEICHA
I won't.

JETA
Promise me.

KEICHA
I'm sorry.

JETA
Promise me.

KEICHA
I promise.

JETA
This time you were lucky. Next time, who knows?

KEICHA
Don't be angry.

JETA (*Considered*)
I'm not angry. You're safe, that's all that matters. Are you cold?

Keicha shakes her head.

JETA
We need more blankets. I'll get us extra blankets. I'll speak to Carl.

KEICHA
(*On edge*) Jeta?

JETA
Don't worry, there's nothing to worry about. I'm here, your Jeta is here.

Jeta wraps a blanket around Keicha and moves to the TV. She switches it on and the room is flooded in projected snow. We also hear a low hum of white noise.

Scene 3

Evening. Lights go black but quickly come up. Keicha is gone and Hannah now stands over her suitcase with one hand on the lid (mirroring Keicha's stance at the opening of scene 2). Hannah begins unpacking while Jeta stands upstage intently watching her.

JETA
What're you doing?

HANNAH (*Cold*)
Unpacking.

JETA
Do you know why you're here?

HANNAH
This is where they sent me.

Beat.

JETA
What's your name?

HANNAH
Hannah.

JETA
How old are you?

HANNAH
Eighteen.

JETA
School?

HANNAH
I finished.

JETA
You *finished* school? You completed your exams?

Hannah nods.

JETA
Did you do well? Were you a good student?

Hannah shrugs.

JETA
Where're your parents?

Hannah doesn't respond.

JETA
I asked you a question. Where're your/

HANNAH
I don't know.

JETA
You don't?

Hannah continues unpacking.

JETA
Well, I'm not your mother.

HANNAH
What?

JETA
I'm not your mother.

HANNAH (*Annoyed*)
I know that.

JETA
You're too old. My daughter's sixteen.

HANNAH
Where is she?

Jeta smiles, moves to Hannah's bed and sits.

JETA
This is a good bed, it squeaks a little but that's to be expected. Its seen a lot of action, a lot of people coming and going. The mattress dips in the middle, you'll find yourself rolling into it.

Jeta plucks a photo from the case.

JETA
Your Irish classmates?

Hannah nods.

JETA
These are your friends?

HANNAH
Some of them.

JETA (*Carefully considering the photo*)
This girl, by your side, she's your friend. See how easily she bends toward you, her head tilted toward yours. But this girl smirking at the camera is your enemy. I bet she didn't call you *Hannah*. She pinned another name on you. What was it?

Hannah snaps the photo from Jeta and lays it on the bed.

JETA (*Laughs*)
Look at all the things you managed to stuff inside your suitcase! You've done this before. Many times, perhaps? You know how to pack up your life in a minute.

Jeta reaches into the case for the alarm clock and picks it up. Hannah tries to snatch it from her but Jeta holds onto it. The alarm suddenly goes off ringing unnaturally loud. They freeze, holding onto the clock and eventually it stops ringing. They both still hold it.

JETA
That's alarming. (*Pointed*) Time to wake up.

Hannah aggressively pulls the alarm clock away from Jeta.

HANNAH
You're wearing my dress.

JETA (*Flat*)
Am I.

HANNAH
I knew this would happen.

JETA
You knew?

HANNAH
When they sent ahead my case.

JETA
Perhaps I borrowed it.

HANNAH
Without asking?

JETA
You want it back? Ask me to take it off.

HANNAH (*Immediately*)
Take it off.

Jeta stands and moves downstage.

JETA (*Smiles*)
I was thinking about my daughter. Perhaps, you remind me of her. Although, that's not true, I'm always thinking about her, can't recall a time when I'm not/

HANNAH
Take off my dress.

JETA
Do you have children?

HANNAH (*Biting*)
And my jewellery.

JETA
You're eighteen. I'd my daughter at that age/

Hannah moves to her, roughly unclasps the necklace and pulls the bracelets from Jeta's wrists. Jeta doesn't protest or struggle.

JETA (*Calm*)
Are you going to strip me?

Hannah moves back to her bed and puts the jewellery inside its box.

JETA
Where're you from?

HANNAH (*Blunt*)
Here.

JETA (*Scoffs*)
Don't fool yourself.

HANNAH
I'm from *here*.

JETA Then why are you in this room with me?

Hannah doesn't respond.

JETA
How'd you get to Ireland?

Hannah doesn't respond.

JETA
When did you arrive? Two, three years ago?

HANNAH (*Sharp*)
Five.

JETA
You're here long enough to forget your accent, (*Smiles*) long enough to pretend to forget. I remember everything. Ask me anything, I'll tell you. Go ahead, ask me, I'll answer.

HANNAH (*Looks toward Keisha's bed*)
Who's there?

JETA Where?

HANNAH (*Tense*)
Whose bed is that?

JETA
Her name is Keicha.

Jeta moves to Keicha's bed and sits.

JETA
She has two pillows. She sleeps with one beneath her head and one between her knees.

HANNAH
Keicha?

JETA

She must sleep with the TV switched on. Always. The white noise settles her, helps her drift off.

HANNAH

How can *I* sleep with the TV on?

JETA

You can sleep during the day.

HANNAH

And sit up all night?

JETA

There's little else to do here. It'll pass the time. You'll get used to it.

HANNAH

What if I *can't* get used to it?

JETA

You could be transferred to another room/

HANNAH (*Angry*)

I'm not moving again! Why should I? I've the same rights here as everyone else!

JETA

That's not how it works.

HANNAH

I won't be pushed about!

JETA *(Patient)*
Would you do something for me?

HANNAH
Why should I?

JETA
Come here, sit beside me.

HANNAH
Take off my dress!

JETA
Don't worry, I'll return it.

HANNAH
Now!

JETA
Soon, I promise. *(Smiles)* Sit here, I don't bite.

HANNAH
I don't want to sit down.

JETA
You mean, you're not ready.

HANNAH
I know what *I* mean.

Hannah returns to her suitcase.

JETA
Do you like games?

HANNAH
What?

JETA
Games. Do you like playing them?

HANNAH
I'm not a child.

JETA
Not all games are for children.

HANNAH
You mean *mind games*, crawling inside someone's head and fucking with them.

JETA
We don't play those games here.

HANNAH
What games do *you* play?

JETA
Please, sit here. I just want to talk.

HANNAH
About what?

JETA (*Indicating the space beside her*)
Please.

Hannah hesitates but decides to sit beside Jeta.

HANNAH (*Blunt*)
Well?

JETA
Let's start over? My name's Jeta.

HANNAH
Jeta?

Jeta holds out her hand and Hannah tentatively takes it.

JETA
You're freezing.

HANNAH
It's cold.

Hannah awkwardly pulls her hand away from Jeta.

JETA
Are you hungry? I've some buns.

HANNAH
That's against the rules.

JETA (*Smiles*)
Don't worry, I won't tell.

HANNAH
I'm not hungry.

JETA
Did you travel far to get here?

HANNAH
Three hours.

JETA
You must be tired?

HANNAH
I'm all right.

JETA
Where did you come from? Dublin?

Hannah nods.

JETA
Did you like it there?

Hannah shrugs.

JETA
It's different here. When I first arrived it took me a long time to adjust. There's nothing to do, the nearest village is four miles away.

HANNAH (*Arrogant*)
I'm not worried about that.

JETA
You're not?

HANNAH
I won't be here long.

JETA
That's what I thought when I arrived *six years ago*. Keisha's been here eight years.

HANNAH (*Determined*)
They're clearing the backlog.

JETA
That's what they say and then kick that can down the road.

HANNAH (*Strong*)
You don't know what's happening *out there/*

JETA
No one knows we're here, to them we're invisible.

HANNAH
I marched, seen the protests, people are sick of it. They've had enough.

JETA
You're a clever girl, I can tell. That's why I'm talking to you like this/

HANNAH (*Aggressive*)
You're doing me a favour, is that it?

JETA
I'm telling you how to survive here.

HANNAH
Survive?

JETA
By helping others.

HANNAH
You want money, is that it?

JETA (*Taken aback*)
I'm talking about supporting each other/

HANNAH (*Distain*)
I don't care about anyone else! Why should I? I look out for myself so stay out of my way!

JETA (*Laughs*)
Stay out of your way? *Here*, in this room? What should I do? Climb out the window?

HANNAH (*Squaring up to Jeta*)
You can crawl under the *fucking bed*!

Jeta and Hannah consider each other intensely. Hannah suddenly stands and moves toward the door.

JETA
Where're you going?

HANNAH (*Stopping at the door*)
Nowhere.

JETA
You've a quick temper.

HANNAH (*Flat*)
Have I.

JETA
That isn't necessarily a bad thing. Although, not everyone here is like me, there're people here who fight all the time. They don't know what else to do, their frustration overpowers them.

HANNAH
I can take care of myself.

JETA
Perhaps you're fighting so long, you can't see when someone reaches out in friendship.

HANNAH (*Disbelief*)
By stealing my clothes? By telling me *I'm* stuck here forever?

JETA
Not forever, everything comes to an end.

HANNAH
What?

Jeta moves to her bedside locker and retrieves a letter. She moves to Hannah and holds it out.

JETA
Go ahead, read it.

Hannah hesitates but takes the letter and reads it.

HANNAH
The 27th? That's...

JETA
Tuesday week.

HANNAH
What're you going to do?

JETA
What can I do?

Jeta takes back her letter and considers it.

HANNAH
I'm... I'm sorry.

JETA
What for? It's not your fault. The truth is, it's almost a relief. Not knowing – *waiting*... anxiety builds and swallows every minute.

HANNAH
You can appeal?

JETA
I've reached the end of the line.

HANNAH
You'll see your family again? Your daughter?

Jeta shakes her head.

HANNAH
Will you have somewhere to stay?

Jeta shrugs.

HANNAH
What's waiting for you back there?

JETA (*Tentative*)
I can't think of that, can't allow myself to think of it. Not yet. All I can do is make sure the people I care for are looked after.

HANNAH
Keicha?

Jeta returns the letter to her bedside locker.

JETA
My father was a painter, there were always canvasses scattered about our home. As a little girl, I'd stand before them watching the paint dry. He specialized in landscape, the plains at dawn, sunset. One day, I tried to jump into one of his paintings. I'd been watching it for hours (*Laughs*) or minutes, who knows how time works for a child?

Jeta moves to Hannah's bed and sits beside her.

JETA
I thought I could see the animals moving, a small herd of elephants moving slowly through the bush. I took three steps back and ran at it holding up my arms like I was diving into a swimming pool. I plunged headfirst through the canvass and the frame shattered. It seemed to me the world had exploded. I cracked my head and broke my wrist but the strange thing was for just a moment, I thought I'd succeed. This is where Keicha resides, beneath the rubble, half way between here and there, scraping the paint from her face, wiping the glass from her eyes.

HANNAH
She's confused about *where* she is?

JETA
That's one way to put it.

HANNAH
Then she needs help.

JETA
That's why I'm talking to you like this/

HANNAH
Professional help.

JETA
She won't go down that road.

HANNAH
Why?

JETA
There's no one here she trusts.

HANNAH
Only you?

Jeta nods.

HANNAH
Does she know about the letter?

JETA
It just arrived today.

HANNAH
So, she doesn't know?

JETA
Not yet.

HANNAH
How'll she take it?

Jeta shrugs.

HANNAH
Is she dangerous?

JETA
Not now but when I arrived she was like a wildcat. My first night here, I woke to find her dragging me from my bed. She was terrified trying to look everywhere at once, hissing at me *to escape*. I guessed she was having a nightmare so, I played along letting her pull me around the room. Eventually, she settled down and I put her back to bed. She told me, the chains are too strong. I sat up with her, making up silly little stories until she drifted off.

HANNAH
You want me to babysit her, is that it? After you're gone?

JETA
I want to teach you a game.

HANNAH
What game?

JETA
It's not difficult, all you've to do is play along.

HANNAH
I've my own problems, I can't take on caring for someone.

JETA
What problems? How'd you get to Ireland? What happened after you arrived?

HANNAH (*Agitated*)
Nothing...

JETA
Please understand, no judgement waits to pounce on you here, Hannah.

Beat.

HANNAH
I'm... I'm hungry.

JETA
Of course you are, you must be starving.

Jeta fetches the buns from her locker.

JETA
These will keep you going.

Hannah hesitates.

JETA
Go on. It's all right.

Jeta offers Hannah the buns and she chooses one.

JETA (*Handing Hannah a bottle of water*)
Here, drink this, it's fresh water.

HANNAH
Thanks.

JETA
I wish I could offer you something more. And the sad truth is the canteen food isn't much better. Their kitchens are run for profit so, they serve us the cheapest muck – frozen pizzas, burgers.

HANNAH
I'm a vegetarian.

JETA
Good luck with that.

HANNAH (*Sharp*)
What am I supposed to eat?

JETA
If you're hungry, you'll eat.

HANNAH
I can't start eating meat/

JETA
Be careful, Hannah. You won't get much mileage from self-pity here.

HANNAH
I'm not feeling sorry for myself.

JETA (*Upbeat*)
Good. Because today is your lucky day.

HANNAH
It is?

JETA
Of course, it is.

HANNAH
Doesn't feel like it.

JETA
Trust me, you arrived at just the right time.

HANNAH
Why's that?

JETA
I'm clearing out my locker, all my treasures. I can't take everything with me.

Jeta moves back to her locker.

HANNAH
All your *treasures*?

JETA
And there's one I think you'll enjoy.

Jeta retrieves a book from her locker and hands it to Hannah.

HANNAH
This is for me?

Jeta nods.

HANNAH (*Suspicious*)
Why?

JETA
Well, you were good enough to lend me your dress.

HANNAH
Without knowing it.

Hannah inspects the well-thumbed novel.

HANNAH (*Unimpressed*)
Moby Dick?

JETA
Have you read it?

HANNAH
No.

JETA
Well, this is your chance.

HANNAH
Is it any good?

JETA
Usually when people receive a gift they say *thank you*.

HANNAH
Thanks. (*Flat*) Is it any good?

JETA
Good? Well, it's one of those stories where I didn't believe in the characters. I didn't believe in them as living breathing people. Captain Ahab is too absurd and the sailors are almost indistinguishable.

HANNAH (*Ironic*)
Sounds great.

JETA
But I believed in their adventure, in the quest for the whale. It taught me something about evil, about the wrong way to fight it. And I think by the time you finish this book, your time here will also be done.

HANNAH
Is this a kind of blackmail?

JETA
Blackmail?

HANNAH
You want me to nurse your friend, hold her hand after you're gone. What about the other women here, her other friends?

JETA
They're prejudiced against her.

HANNAH
You mean they don't like her.

JETA
They don't know her like I do.

HANNAH
Thanks for offering me your book, Jeta. But I won't be in your debt.

Hannah holds out the book but Jeta refuses to take it.

JETA
You're not in my debt/

HANNAH (*Strong*)
If I want to read *Moby Dick*, I'll buy it myself.

JETA
How about I'm in *your* debt if you accept it?

HANNAH
How's that?

JETA
Maybe you'll think of me from time-to-time when you read it.

HANNAH
What benefit is that to you?

JETA (*Smiles*)
Think of it as vanity. It's comforting to think I've left my mark on the place.

HANNAH (*Stubborn*)
I don't like the idea of you owing me anything either.

JETA
Then give *me* something.

HANNAH
What?
JETA
Trade for it. Give me something in return and then we're even.

HANNAH (*Considered*)
All right, keep the dress.

JETA
No...

HANNAH
It's no use to me here? Anyway, you'll get the weather for it.

JETA
It's too much!

HANNAH
That's the deal.

JETA
Well, if *that's* the deal, then that's the *deal*.

Hannah places the book inside her locker.

JETA
You're independent.

HANNAH (*Flat*)
Am I.

JETA
But you can't cut yourself off from where you are, Hannah.

HANNAH (*Snaps*)
I know that.

JETA
I've seen women try, they drift about here like they're in a dream. But sooner or later something happens and their whole world comes crashing down.

HANNAH *(Blunt)*
I've seen the world crash down and I'm still here.

Hannah returns to unpacking her suitcase as Jeta watches her. We suddenly hear a door slam, a baby crying and voices raised in anger. Blackout.

Scene 4

Morning. The lights snap up finding Carl kneeling by the radiator. Jeta stands watching Carl bleed the pipes.

JETA (*Upbeat*)
... I was in the middle of my dinner, Anias towering over me. Said, she wanted to speak with me *in private*. She's an intimidating woman, Carl. And I thought I'd upset her.

CARL
She can be very... very intense.

JETA (*Laughs*)
That's the understatement of the century!

CARL
What did she want?

JETA
Well, this is it. She practically dragged me out to the garden, kept looking around as though we were being followed. It was getting dark and I can tell you, I was sweating.

But she didn't want to punch me, she wanted to tell me they're poisoning us in the canteen.

CARL (*Digesting this*)
Right...

JETA
Told me, they poison the food.

CARL
What did you say?

JETA
I said, that explains the taste.

CARL
She was joking?

JETA
That's what I thought but then I noticed how thin she is. She saw Nora sprinkle a fine white powder into a pot. I told her it was salt. But she looked at me like I was crazy. Said, that's what they want us to think. She said, they're giving us cancer.

CARL (*Shocked*)
Cancer?

JETA
Her little boy clung to her leg. He's so thin, Carl. I think she's afraid to give him the food.

CARL
Don't worry, I'll talk to her.

JETA
What'll you say?

CARL
I'll... I'll eat the food with her. Or bring her into the kitchen and she can taste the salt, watch Nora make the dinners. I don't know... whatever. Have to say it's a new one on me. I haven't come across it before.

JETA
All she wants is to cook her own food.

CARL
I know that, Jeta. But what can we do? We all have to play the game.

Jeta appears unsatisfied.

CARL (*Changing the subject*)
Did you tell Keicha yet?

Jeta sighs.

CARL
What did she say?

JETA
She hasn't spoken to me since.

CARL
Why?

JETA
She thinks I betrayed her or I've disappointed her. It's difficult to explain.

CARL
It's a lot to take in, the idea of you leaving.

JETA
Yeah...

CARL
Is she gone out?

JETA
Gone *walking* to the village. She won't take the bus anymore. Waiting at the stop with the others, the way people look at them, said, she feels like a panda in the zoo.

CARL
People round here love a good gawk.

JETA
Perhaps, you'll watch over her for me?

CARL
Don't worry, I'll keep an eye on her.

JETA
Thanks.

CARL
Have you made arrangements for arriving in Harare?

JETA
I expect to be... well, to be picked up.

CARL
By family?

JETA (*Laughs*)
I wish. No, I mean questioned, arrested by the police.

CARL
Arrested?

JETA
Over there I'm a fugitive, Carl. An anarchist. It's hard to imagine now but you should've seen me in my prime. I spoke out and people listened.

CARL
About what?

JETA
Vote rigging, repression of the media, LGBT rights, social inequality. You name it, I'd something to say about it. Of course, we were branded anarchists, only interested in looting and violence. That was the charge I spent my first period in prison for.

CARL
Looting?

JETA (*Laughing at Carl's shocked expression*)
Looting and arson.

CARL (*Stunned*)
You think you know someone!

JETA
I don't know why I'm laughing, I certainly wasn't then. Of course, that's what they charged everyone with - looting, arson, civil disobedience, obstructing justice. They sent in their heavies to infiltrate our peaceful protests, they turned them violent and gave Mugabe an excuse to ignore our demands.

CARL
You never told me any of this.

JETA

No one talks about their past here, Carl. There's a general fear of being watched or evaluated. Or terrified what you'll say, opening old wounds. (*Sighs*) But now, I've to face it all again anyway.

CARL

Your daughter? You mentioned her to me once. Is she in Harare?

JETA (*Flustered*)

No, she lives in America, Chicago. It's... it's a long story.

CARL

I'm sorry, Jeta.

JETA

No, it's all right. I'm grateful really, I'm grateful Kessie's safe.

CARL (*Apologetic*)

I didn't mean to stick my nose in.

JETA

No... no, I like talking about her.

CARL

Is she with family?

JETA

She's with her father - Simon, my ex-husband.

CARL
When did you last see her?

JETA
In person?

Carl nods.

JETA
Before my final stretch in prison, nine years ago. I was picked up a month before local elections, they rounded up all the *troublemakers*. Pulled me out of the university, right in the middle of a lecture. She was seven... beautiful really, and funny. See this birthmark? (*Jeta points to a birthmark on her cheek*) She has one just like it. We call them our face-maps, a map from her face to mine. Anyway, this time when I was picked up the charge was more serious. I contacted Simon and asked him to take Kessie.

CARL
He didn't mind?

JETA
He was delighted! Simon's a good man but we went through an ugly divorce. I suppose my activism played a part. He thought I was making unnecessary trouble for us, for our little family. I thought I was making a better world for my daughter. Of course, he also believed I was interested in someone else. Maybe he was right.

CARL
He took her to America?

JETA
He's an experienced engineer and received a job offer and visa to work there. I didn't know how my trial would go so, when he sent papers to sign, I didn't hesitate. I thought she'd return after I was released. But... but well, I didn't hear from them for three months. That wasn't Simon's fault, he got me out of jail, bribed the police before they left and after the elections I made bail. When we *did* speak, it was obvious she settled there... she was happy. I knew if I didn't leave too, I'd end up back in jail. So, I skipped bail and got out of there.

CARL
But you're still in contact?

JETA (*Nods*)
She's sixteen now, an A student. (*Smiles*) She speaks with an American accent. Simon remarried and they've a child, a little boy. Kessie was planning a trip to visit me after I received my papers. Of course, that'll never happen now.

CARL
I don't know what to say, Jeta.

JETA
Believe me, every night I count my blessings.

CARL
You do?

JETA (*Defiant*)
I know my daughter is safe. I see her in my mind's eye in Chicago, living a decent life and having opportunities. I look at Keicha and count my lucky stars. Her daughter simply walked out the door one summer's evening, off to meet a boy and never came home.

CARL
I didn't know that.

JETA
She believes Boko Haram are responsible, at that time a number of local girls had disappeared. But she'll never know for certain.

CARL
Can't imagine going... going through something like that.

JETA
Believe me, Carl, that's just one of the crosses she carries, that we share and carry together.

CARL
She'll miss you, that's for sure. I know you kept each other going.

JETA
Hopefully Hannah can... can be of some comfort to her.

CARL
How's she settling in?

JETA
It's too early to tell.

Jeta moves to the open suitcase.

JETA
First thing every morning, she packs it and unpacks it last thing at night.

CARL
Why?

JETA (*Shrugs*)
We all have our ways of staying sane here. Maybe it's her way of remembering she's only passing through. She gave me this dress.

CARL
She did?

JETA (*Smiles*)
Didn't you notice?

CARL (*Flustered*)
Of course...

JETA
Well, do you like it?

CARL
It's... it's very nice on you, lovely now. I wish we'd the weather for it.

JETA
Perhaps, we'll get closer before I leave. I'd like that. There are things I can teach her, things that'll make it easier for her here.

CARL
I wanted to talk to you about that. I made a few phone calls, chanced my arm. But I got a contact through the parish priest.

JETA
A contact?

CARL
Of another priest working in Harare - Fr. Michael Kinavan. Very well respected over there by all accounts, bit of a legend. Runs a mission, been over there twenty years.

JETA
What about him?

CARL
Well, I rang and told him about you.

JETA
About me? What did you say?

CARL
Just about how... how you cared for people here, led by example.

JETA (*Amused*)
Is that what I've done?

CARL (*Smiles*)
Well, yeah, basically I lied. I wanted to run it by you but... but he's eager to meet you, willing to meet you off the plane.

JETA
He is?

CARL
I wanted to run it by you first. And if you feel there's going to be trouble with the authorities, he could definitely help. I was talking to him and he's completely sound, he knows the score over there. I know he could help, he's definitely willing and in a position to... to help.

JETA
One problem.

CARL
What's that?

JETA
I'm not Catholic.

CARL
Sure, who's Catholic these days?

JETA
The Pope?

CARL (*Laughs*)
You got me there.

JETA
Thanks for... for trying to help.

CARL
All I did was make a few phone calls.

JETA
Still, I appreciate it.

CARL (*Frustrated*)
I can't believe... it's hard to believe your application was refused, Jeta. I don't know who makes these decisions. I'd love them to work here for a week, for them to see what I see. I wish there was more I could do.

JETA (*Hesitant*)
Maybe, there is. I... I wasn't sure I'd be brave enough or you'd understand. But if I ask you to do something, something extreme, would you consider it?

CARL (*Worried*)
What is it?

JETA
Transfer Keicha to another centre, after I'm gone.

CARL
Why?

JETA
Please, Carl transfer her to a *women* only centre. After what she's been through with men, they've a control over her, she gives in to whatever they demand.

CARL
That doesn't sound like the person I know.

JETA
What?

CARL
Well, she's never been shy putting her foot down with me.

JETA
That's because she doesn't see you as *a man*.

CARL (*Ironic*)
Thank you.

JETA
She thinks of you as an awkward father.

CARL
She said that? A father?

JETA
An awkward one.

CARL
But if she's here, I can keep an eye on her.

JETA
24 hours a day? Seven days a week?

CARL
You know I can't do that.

JETA
Then please, consider my request.

CARL
What're you afraid of?

JETA
There are men here, Carl, men who want to get their hooks in her. I've kept them at bay as best I can. But after I'm gone Keicha will have no one to protect her.

CARL
What men? Who are they? (*Strong*) Who are they, Jeta?

Jeta shakes her head.

CARL (*Exasperated*)
You want to tell me their names. Why else bring it up?

JETA
Ray Okonjo, Lukeson Solarin and Anthony Aguda. They prey on women here by getting them into debt.

CARL
How?

JETA
They lend money, give it away at first as though it's nothing. Then, when they're certain the women can't repay, they rent rooms in Cork and have them work it off.

CARL
Selling sex?

JETA
You remember the night Keicha broke curfew?

CARL
She went to a birthday in Cork.

JETA
That's what she says.

CARL
You don't believe her?

Jeta shakes her head.

CARL (*Angry*)
Why didn't you tell me this before?

JETA
These men, Carl, they're very dangerous. They've many friends. I know how they operate, I've seen first-hand what they're capable of. But you can get Keicha out of here.

CARL
I can't transfer someone just like that.

JETA
She needs a fresh start, a place to start over.

CARL
Then I should transfer every woman here!

JETA
What?

CARL
If one woman isn't safe, none of them are.

JETA
So what can you do?

CARL
Get the Guards in! Those lads will be out of here before they can blink!

JETA (*Heated*)
There are other men involved, men who aren't residents here. Don't you see? It doesn't matter who gets arrested or transferred, those men know Keicha is here.

CARL (*Snaps*)
I can't believe you never told me this!

JETA
Perhaps, I can't believe you didn't see it happening under your nose.

CARL
This is my fault?

JETA
Keep people in a state of poverty and they'll commit desperate acts.

CARL
I don't control that!

JETA (*Patient*)
I'm not blaming you, Carl. I'm simply asking you to consider my request. That's all I ask, that you think it over. You do your best here, everyone knows that. *I* know it.

CARL
Right...

Carl moves to leave.

JETA
Where are you going?

CARL
Where do you think? I'm calling the Guards.

JETA
What're you going to tell them?

CARL
About those scumbags!

JETA (*Panicked*)
But you can't! Not yet! They'll know I was the informer!

CARL
How could they know?

JETA
Trust me, they'll find out. Please, wait a few days, I'll have left and they'll be unable to reach me.

CARL
They can't hurt you here.

JETA
You don't know what they're capable of, Carl. And, you see, behind all my fine words I'm really a coward.

CARL
You're not a coward, Jeta.

JETA
It's certainly what I've become.

CARL (*Firm*)
You're not a coward.

JETA
Of course I am. That's why I didn't tell you about this sooner.

Carl moves downstage.

JETA (*On edge*)
What'll you do?

CARL (*Fuming*)
All right, I'll wait.

JETA (*Relieved*)
Thank you.

CARL
The second you're safe, I'll deal with them. Ray Okonjo... I should've seen it. What other women are involved?

JETA
I don't know.

CARL
Jeta?

JETA
I don't know.

CARL
Keicha will?

JETA
She won't talk about it, she denies it even to me. She's not in control of this, that's why she needs someone to step in and give her an exit.

CARL
I'll think about it... we'll see how she goes, when the dust settles. That's all I can promise.

JETA
That's all I ask.

Beat.

CARL
Right, better get back to the desk.

JETA
Oh, wait! Before I forget, I got you something.

CARL (*Distracted*)
What's that?

JETA
I wanted to give you something. A parting gift.

CARL
There's no need, Jeta.

Jeta moves to her bedside locker and retrieves the gift.

JETA
There's no need for anything, I wanted to. Don't get too excited, it's just a short letter of thanks and a little painting.

Jeta hands over the present and Carl considers the painting.

CARL
Did you paint it?

JETA (*Nods*)
So you've to pretend to like it.

CARL
What is it?

JETA (*Mock disgust*)
What is it?

CARL
I mean, what's it of?

JETA
Can't you tell?

CARL
A flock of birds?

JETA (*Considered*)
A flock of birds.

CARL
Am I right?

JETA
If that's what you see, then that's what it is.

CARL
We'll talk later, sort out those arrangements with Fr. Kinavan.

JETA
All right.

CARL
Wrap up if you're going out, they're forecasting snow. Can you believe it? Almost April and they're forecasting snow.

JETA
I used to think it was made-up, just something in fairy-tales.

CARL
Snow?

JETA
I'd draw snowmen and hang the pictures above my bed. Now, I see it here, out there and yet somehow, I still don't believe in it.

Jeta moves to stand before Carl.

JETA
Why is that, Carl?

CARL
I don't know, Jeta.

Jeta reaches out to caress Carl's cheek. We hear a distinct scratching like fingernails scraped across plasterboard. Blackout.

Scene 5

Evening. The lights snap up revealing Keicha with one hand on the lid (mirroring her stance at the opening of scene 2) of a new suitcase placed on Jeta's bed. Keicha's bed has been turned over and sits on its side. The scratching sounds fade as Keicha investigates the new suitcase finding a wash bag, a woolly hat, a set of rosary beads and finally, an old rag doll. She holds the doll up to the light.

KEICHA (*Mumbling to the doll*)
Look at you! Aren't you pretty? What's your name? Don't be frightened. There's no reason to be frightened. (*Playful*) Welcome to our little palace. You want to look out the window?

Keicha carries the doll downstage and looks out.

KEICHA
There it is, there's the world. What do you think? (*Smiles*) That bad? Shh... I know, don't cry. You're just tired, that's all is wrong. (*Almost to herself*) You travelled a long way and now you're tired. You need to rest.

Keicha brings the doll back to the suitcase, casually carrying it by the leg and places it inside. She moves to her overturned bed and considers it. Hannah enters carrying a Spar shopping bag. She appears to have aged and her hiking boots are worn and covered in mud.

KEICHA (*Anxious*)
Where were you? Fucking Spar? What took so long?

Hannah doesn't respond.

KEICHA
I was worried. I thought... I thought something happened.

Hannah moves to her bed, sits and looks toward Keicha's overturned bed.

KEICHA (*Unsettled*)
I heard whispering and... and scratching like fingernails scraped across plasterboard. I thought it was one of the children playing a trick – Emmanuel or Michael. But, I turned over the bed, no one was there.

Beat.

KEICHA
What did you buy?

Hannah ignores her and winds up her alarm clock. Keicha moves to the shopping bag and turns it up, a roll of toilet paper and box of chalk drop out. Keicha picks up the chalk box.

KEICHA
What's this?

Hannah snaps the chalk box from her.

KEICHA
Carl dropped off a case.

Hannah moves to the suitcase and inspects it.

KEICHA (*Tentative*)
We didn't talk about you, we talked about his family. They spend their weekends by the sea. There's a mobile home on the coast and every weekend they travel down to it. He takes the twins fishing, he has twin girls. One has asthma and the sea air helps her – it clears her lungs. When the weather permits, they take out a fishing boat. He showed me a picture on his phone, they were standing on a pretty beach holding up their rods.

Keicha moves to the suitcase.

KEICHA (*Secretive*)
I asked him why he didn't wear a wedding ring. You know what he said? *Some men don't.*

Keicha takes the woolly hat from the case and holds it before Hannah.

KEICHA
Try this on. To see if it fits.

Hannah doesn't respond so Keicha roughly plants the hat on her head and pulls it down over her ears.

KEICHA (*Adjusting the hat*)
Hold still!

Hannah violently tears it from her head and throws the hat on the floor. She moves back to the chalk box, removes a stick of white chalk and draws three lines on the floor, neatly dividing the room into three separate segments.

KEICHA
What're you doing?

Hannah finishes dividing the room and sits. Keicha considers the lines, moves to the bed with the suitcase and sits.

KEICHA (*Sincere*)
Hannah, I want us to talk. We've a lot in common, it's strange we don't talk. We've seen the good and bad in life, we've both suffered. We could cry and laugh together. We could pass the time, talk through the days. At night we could hold each other, make up stories and keep each other warm. (*Scared*) Sometimes when I'm here alone, I feel like I'm lost in a dream. I'm foolish and babble on... I know that. But couldn't we spend these days getting to know each other, getting close to each other? I can't stand this silence.

Hannah reacts.

KEICHA
I'm sorry. I didn't mean to upset you. Did I upset you? I swear, I didn't mean to. That's the last thing I want.

Hannah takes a letter from her locker, moves downstage and considers it.

KEICHA
What's that?

HANNAH (*Quiet*)
A letter. She left it for me.

KEICHA
What does it say?

HANNAH (*Reading*)
I'm sorry we didn't have time to become friends. I'm certain we would have. Please consider the things we discussed. I know now I take with me only what I managed to give. It has many names - dignity, compassion, a sense of humanity. But I believe it's called hope. My slender prayer would never have survived in isolation. Perhaps, from time to time, you will think of me. I wish you all the luck in the world.

Keicha reaches out to touch Hannah's shoulder.

HANNAH (*Rigid*)
Don't touch me. Don't *touch* me.

Keicha tenderly touches Hannah's cheeks, eyes, and forehead.

HANNAH (*Quiet*)
I don't want you to do that. I don't want you to be kind to me. Leave me alone! DON'T TOUCH ME!

Hannah pulls away from Keicha, moves to her bed and sits.

HANNAH (*Softly*)
It's time... I have... many times... (*Indicates herself*) wanted to... to... It's sick, it disgusts me and it's always the same. I see it... see it so clearly, sometimes I think it already happened. (*Cruel, to Keicha*) Do you know how much I hate you? Everything about you, everything you do. How've I put up with you so long, never saying a word? My hatred eating me, burning through me. What're you thinking? Perhaps, after all, you prefer my silence.

Keicha appears upset but Hannah quickly moves to her.

HANNAH (*Shocked by her cruelty*)
Keicha... I don't know what I said... I don't know why I say these things. You meant well... I see that now. Please... don't be upset. Please, say you forgive me. (*Timid*) We... we can play the game. She taught me how, she taught me the words. I know what to say.

KEICHA (*Confused*)
Game?

HANNAH
The rhyme... the story.

KEICHA
What story?

HANNAH
She taught me what to say.

KEICHA
I don't understand.

HANNAH
Come here, sit beside me.

Hannah leads Keicha to her bed and they sit.

HANNAH
Now, ask me.

KEICHA
Ask you *what*?

HANNAH
What time is it?

KEICHA
What time is it?

HANNAH
Over *there.*

KEICHA
What time is it over there?

HANNAH
Morning. Now you say - *what kind of day is it?*

KEICHA
What kind of day is it?

HANNAH
Beautiful, the sun is coming up, the morning mist is fading. Now you say - *and the village?* Don't you remember?

KEICHA
Remember?

HANNAH
You say - *and the village?*

KEICHA (*Distracted*)
And... and the...

Keicha stands and moves slowly toward the bed with the suitcase.

HANNAH
What's wrong?

KEICHA
Shhh...

HANNAH
Keicha?

KEICHA (*On edge*)
Can't you hear it?

HANNAH
Hear what?

KEICHA
Whispering... the scratching.

HANNAH
Scratching?

KEICHA
Listen.

Beat.

HANNAH
I can't hear anything.

KEICHA
There!

HANNAH
Where?

KEICHA (*Points to Jeta's bed*)
Under the bed. Listen!

HANNAH (*Frustrated*)
I can't hear anything.

KEICHA
Scratching.

HANNAH
It's mice under the floorboards.

KEICHA
And whispering.

HANNAH
It's the pipes hissing.

KEICHA
No...

Keicha places the suitcase on the floor and takes hold of the bed.

KEICHA
Help me.

HANNAH
What're you doing?

KEICHA
I have to see, I have to know.

HANNAH
Just look under it.

KEICHA
I have to be certain. Help me!

Keicha tries to turn over the bed.

HANNAH
Be careful! You'll break it!

Hannah moves to the bed and takes hold of it.

KEICHA
On the count of three. One!

HANNAH
This is madness.

KEICHA
Two!

HANNAH
There's nothing under here.

KEICHA
Three!

They turn over the bed and there's nothing beneath.

HANNAH
You see?

KEICHA
I was certain...

HANNAH
It was the floorboards creaking, the pipes hissing.

KEICHA
No... *listen.*

We hear a distant scratching and low moaning.

KEICHA
Can't you hear it?

Hannah listens and appears disturbed. The scratching and moaning grow louder.

KEICHA (*Unsettled*)
It's under your bed.

HANNAH (*Terrified*)
No... the walls are thin, it's coming from another room.

The scratching/moaning grow louder and as they approach the bed, Jeta's hand appears from beneath it. Keicha and Hannah freeze. Jeta's hand is perfectly still.

JETA (*Whispering*)
Keicha? Help me... I'm so cold, I can't see. Everything is black, empty. Keicha, are you afraid of me now? Now, I'm dead. I can't sleep, there's no rest, no comfort. I can't leave... I can't leave you. (*Weeping*) I'm so tired. Keicha. Won't you comfort me?

KEICHA (*Upset*)
It's just a dream!

JETA
Perhaps for you but not for me. I'm afraid, hold me until my fear has passed. Please, Keicha, come and comfort me.

HANNAH (*Furious*)
No one would do what you ask! We're alive, we want nothing to do with your death! What you ask is disgusting, no one would do it! You've no right to ask it! No right to speak!

KEICHA (*Transfixed*)
What's it like?

JETA
Your voice is faint, you're so far away, I can't hear you. You must come closer... closer...

Keicha approaches Jeta but stops to look back at Hannah.

JETA (*Weeping*)
Keicha, please... hold my hand. Comfort me... keep me warm. I'm cold.... I'm frightened...

Keicha moves to Jeta.

KEICHA (*Tender*)
I'm here, don't cry. Your Keicha is here.

Keicha knees by Jeta's outstretched hand.

JETA (*Weeping*)
Keicha... touch me... *touch me...*

HANNAH (*Distressed*)
There's spots on her hand, her flesh is rotting! Don't touch her! She has no right to ask it! No right to speak!

Keicha holds Jeta's hand.

JETA
Comfort me... keep me warm... I'm so cold...

Keicha gently strokes Jeta's limp hand but her grip tightens and Keicha appears in pain.

JETA
Closer... closer...

Jeta begins to pull Keicha beneath the bed.

KEICHA (*Panic*)
LET GO! I CAN'T! I CAN'T! LET GO! (*Screams*) HELP ME! HELP ME! HANNAH!

Hannah moves to Keicha and successfully pulls her away from the bed. Jeta's hand becomes still once more.

JETA (*Pleading*)
Keicha... Keicha...

Keicha sits on the floor with her back to Jeta.

KEICHA (*Broken*)
I can't... I can't...

JETA (*Weak*)
Hannah... the dark is all around... touch me... comfort me... take my hand...

HANNAH (*Harsh*)
If I loved you, I could do what you ask. But how could *I* love?

Jeta weeps and slowly withdraws her hand from sight through this section.

HANNAH
You ask for comfort? There's none. Here, your suffering is hollow and has no memory. All your sacrifice has come to nothing, you're sliding off the face of the world with no one to bear witness. All the dead surround you, they can't tell night from day. They are faceless, toothless, blind. You reach out for mercy and beg our pity but you can't feel. You can only tear and wound and hurt/

KEICHA
Stop it!

HANNAH (*Vicious, to Keicha*)
Who're you shouting at?

KEICHA
Leave her be!

HANNAH
Leave *who* be?

Keicha looks toward the bed and finds the hand withdrawn.

HANNAH (*Commanding*)
Get up.

Keicha doesn't move.

HANNAH (*Furious*)
GET FUCKING UP!

Hannah pulls Keicha to her feet.

HANNAH (*Demanding*)
Where are you?

KEICHA
I don't know!

HANNAH (*Defiant*)
A woman with a clipboard came to collect you. She says to follow her – a car is waiting. The driver doesn't talk. You ask, where're you taking me? But he doesn't answer, he doesn't look at you. The woman sits up front, she won't talk. She taps her clipboard with her pen. She points to a bus shelter, they pull in and pick up a man.

KEICHA
A man?

HANNAH
He signs his name on the clipboard and sits in the back. He sits in the back beside you. He *knows*.

KEICHA
Knows what?

HANNAH
The car pulls off, speeding up. The man pushes closer to you letting his hand brush off yours. No one talks, the diver drives, the woman holds her clipboard, the man watches you. Suddenly, he whispers.

KEICHA
What?

HANNAH
He knows. He's a strong man, he has strong hands. You drive along a motorway, you can smell him, he edges closer. You want to sleep, want to lie down and close your eyes. The man pats his lap, he wants you to place your

head in his lap. They pull into a caravan park, there's no one around, the caravan park is dark. Then you see men waiting in the shadows, they're waiting for you. They stand about smoking, someone is laughing. The woman tells you – *you're here.*

KEICHA
Where?

HANNAH
They've been waiting for you, they're excited. The woman holds up her clipboard and the men part, they allow the woman through. You try to follow but they close in around you. They know.

KEICHA (*Angry*)
What do they know!

HANNAH
The man has told them, he's whispering in their ears. At first they're shy – pushing and prodding. You drop your bag, everything spills on the ground.

Keicha appears to hear something, moves to Hannah's bed and looks down on it.

HANNAH
They're excited, they get bolder. The man directs them, they reach out, they've strong hands, they place something inside your mouth. They're ready.

KEICHA (*Distant, considering the bed*)
The things you said... the way you spoke to her. It's unforgivable.

Hannah moves downstage, looks out and speaks silently, mouthing words. Keicha moves around the bed and takes hold of it. She takes a deep breath, building up her courage, and throws over the bed. Jeta is lying in a crumpled heap on the floor.

KEICHA
My heart. My child.

Jeta stands and moves downstage. Keicha opens her arms toward her.

KEICHA
I found you.

Jeta also begins speaking silently, mouthing words as a sound of white noise builds. Lights flare. Blackout.

Scene 6

Morning. Lights snap up and we find Carl listening to Hannah. The room is restored and Hannah's suitcase sits open on the bed.

HANNAH
I'm trying but... but it's difficult. They want housing references and prefer employed tenants. Until I've a permanent address I won't receive social welfare. So, I can't afford a deposit.

CARL (*Sighs*)
That's what happens.

HANNAH
I'm free to stay in this country but now, nowhere will take me.

CARL
Where do you want to live?

HANNAH
Dublin.

CARL
What's the story with rent?

HANNAH
A one bedroom is about two hundred and thirty a week.

CARL
How much rent allowance will you get?

HANNAH
I'm not sure. Fifty or sixty, depending.

CARL
If you're claiming social welfare that won't leave you much. Will it leave you anything?

HANNAH
More than I'm used to.

CARL
Throw in food, heat, electricity – it adds up.

HANNAH
I know that.

CARL
You can stay here?

HANNAH
No.

CARL
Just until everything's sorted. It happens all the time, gives people a little space to get set up.

HANNAH
Thank you but... but I don't want that.

CARL
You got somewhere to stay?

HANNAH (*Definite*)
I booked a hostel.

CARL
In Dublin?

Hannah nods.

CARL
Well, I can give you a reference. Go to the letting agent and tell them the deal. Get them to ring me and I'll vouch for you.

HANNAH
Will it do any good?

CARL
If they're decent they'll set up a meeting between you and the landlord. They'll call and I'll back you up. After that, it's up to you.

HANNAH
Thanks.

CARL
You can always go through the newspapers, skip the agents and deal with a landlord directly. It works out better for most people and besides, you can work. You'll pick up a job handy enough. You've friends in town?

HANNAH
People I went to school with. We haven't been in touch for a while.

CARL
You still have their numbers?

HANNAH
From the last time we spoke.

CARL
When was that?

HANNAH (*Tight*)
It's been awhile... before I arrived.

CARL
Well, I've a list of agencies can help you find your feet. Just call them and arrange an appointment. They're amazing people, they'll do anything for you, help you find work.

HANNAH
I'd like to go to college.

CARL (*Smiles*)
Oh yeah? What would you like to study?

HANNAH
There's a course - Law and Social Movements. It looks at how a global movement of people can shape domestic policy.

CARL
Well, they'll know all about that. I've the list in the office, they'll help you find something. You can phone them from here if you like.

HANNAH
Thanks.

CARL
How're you getting to Dublin?

HANNAH
The bus.

CARL
What time?

HANNAH
Twelve.

CARL
You'll want to say your goodbyes?

HANNAH
Yeah.

CARL
I'll be in the office.

HANNAH
All right.

CARL
Drop in and make that call before… before you go.

Carl turns to leave.

HANNAH
Can I ask you a question?

CARL
Of course.

HANNAH
Are you married?

CARL (*Slightly taken aback*)
Married?

HANNAH
Do you've a wife?

CARL
Well...

HANNAH
You don't have to answer.

CARL (*Awkward*)
No... well, I'm not married.

HANNAH
I see.

CARL
There is someone... a partner, I suppose.

HANNAH
Do you've children?

CARL
No... no children, not yet. Why do you ask?

HANNAH
What happened to Keicha?

CARL (*Cautious*)
That was a long time ago/

HANNAH
What happened to her?

CARL (*Considered*)
Keicha was transferred to Ballyhaunis/

HANNAH
I know that. But *why*?

CARL
She was finding it difficult here, Hannah. I mean... well, you saw what she did to the room, destroyed the place. The powers that be wanted me to call in the Guards, have her charged with vandalism. I just managed to keep them out of it/

HANNAH
She needed help

CARL
There's professional help available, she refused it. You can't force someone to seek treatment.

HANNAH
It's a form of punishment.

CARL
What is?

HANNAH
Transferring people like that.

CARL
She was finding it difficult here, Hannah/

HANNAH
So you dump her somewhere else.

CARL
I didn't *dump* her anywhere.

Frustrated, Hannah moves downstage and looks out.

CARL
Keicha is still in the system, Hannah. They've streamlined the application process, it's going to make a big difference. Anyway, she can work now, get out of the centre and she may receive her papers any day.

HANNAH
It's too late.

CARL
Too late?

HANNAH
For Jeta.

CARL
Jeta's application was refused.

HANNAH
Why?

CARL
She failed to prove her case, you know all this/

HANNAH (*Upset*)
Why was I believed? Why wasn't I sent packing?

CARL
Hannah/

HANNAH
Do you know what the greatest injustice is? Patience missing its reward. Her one enduring wish to leave here simply as you do.

CARL
It's not that straight forward. There has to be some kind of system in place.

HANNAH
She was kept here for years, scraping by and for what crime? If that makes us victims, what does it make you?

CARL
The system isn't perfect, everyone knows that. They're working hard to improve it, speed things up, allow people to work/

HANNAH
It's too late.

CARL
Not for you. Your new life is just beginning. You can put all this behind you.

HANNAH
Just like that?

CARL
You've been given a chance, an opportunity here/

HANNAH
But they won't leave me alone.

CARL
Who won't?

HANNAH
Keisha... the way I treated her... Jesus, the way I treated her.

CARL
You did your best under difficult circumstances.

HANNAH
Did I? I shut her out, treated her like a ghost. Didn't talk to her, wouldn't even look at her.

CARL
You did what you had to, to... to get by.

HANNAH
She needed someone and... and I was here.

CARL
Listen to me, Hannah. She wasn't your responsibility.

HANNAH
That's *why* I should've did something. That's what Jeta tried to tell me – I *take* from here only what I can *give/*

CARL
You can't think like that. Thinking like that will hold you here, stop you from moving on.

HANNAH
But they won't leave me alone.

CARL
Who won't?

HANNAH
They reach out to me, calling me closer. They're here right now, Jeta sitting on her bed, Keicha standing by the case. Can't you see them?

CARL
I see *you*, Hannah. A young woman with her whole life ahead of her. It's going to take time... it's going to take some time to adjust.

Beat.

CARL
I'll be in the office, I'll wait for you in the office. You can make those phone calls, I have that list.

Carl moves to Hannah.

CARL
I think about them too.

HANNAH
You do?

CARL
All the time. Please, Hannah, call in and see me before... before you go.

Hannah nods and Carl exits. She moves to the locker, retrieves her copy of Moby Dick and flicks through it. Keicha/ Jeta enter and sit on their beds. Eventually, Hannah places the book inside her suitcase.

KEICHA
Hannah?

HANNAH (*To herself*)
When I was a little girl, my mother would dress me up. After a hot bath, she'd dress me up like I was her doll.

JETA
Hannah?

HANNAH
My father was a painter. There were always canvasses scattered about our home. As a little girl, I'd stand before them watching the paint dry.

Hannah picks up her alarm clock and considers it. Keicha and Jeta speak directly to Hannah. Hannah continues packing her suitcase through this section.

KEICHA (*Upbeat*)
What time is it over there?

JETA
Morning.

KEICHA
What kind of day is it?

JETA
Beautiful.

KEICHA
Tell me.

JETA
The sun is up. The morning mist is fading.

KEICHA
And the village?

JETA

Is waking up. Jeleel stretches outside his home. He's singing, his mother is swaying. His voice carries and everyone hears it.

KEICHA
And the children?

JETA

Are dressed and ready for school. Their uniforms are clean and ironed, their white shirts gleaming in the sun.

KEICHA
They're happy.

Jeta and Keicha stand.

JETA

There'll be a celebration tonight. Everyone is excited preparing the feast.

KEICHA
And the village?

JETA

Is calling home its children. They returned from far away to join the celebrations. There are tears of welcome, presents and stories are exchanged. (*Smiles*) Umara throws a bright cape over his grandmother's shoulders and everyone laughs. She chases the children, gathering them up in her cape.

KEICHA
And the village?

Keicha and Jeta move to stand directly behind Hannah.

HANNAH
Is full of music, the musicians have arrived. Everyone surrounds them and the village breathes. The fire is its heart, the doorways are its eyes, our song is its voice. When the music stops, we walk hand-in-hand home to bed. We drift off to sleep and the village is at peace.

As Hannah places her hand on the suitcase's lid (mirroring Keicha's stance at the opening of Scene 2) Keicha and Jeta each place a hand on Hannah's shoulder. They freeze in these positions as the lights fade. Blackout.

-------------------------- END --------------------------

Who You Are and What You Do

by Hugh Dichmont

Cast & Creatives

Who You Are and What You Do by Hugh Dichmont was first performed at The Bread & Roses Theatre from 22nd March to 2nd April 2022, with the following cast and creatives:

Cast:

MARIA / CLOWNIER
Valeria Rodríguez

TOM / JOHN
James Heatlie

HUGO / ACORN
Evan L. Barker

SANDY / FATIMA / VISION & VOICE OF BERNADETTE
Mohana Rajagopal

GEORGE / DANIEL
Tosin Olomowewe

PATRICIA / SIRI / KAREN
Kate Sketchley

<u>Creatives:</u>

Director
Tom Ward

Producer
Natalie Chan

Creative Producers
Rebecca Pryle & Velenzia Spearpoint

Assistant Director & Producer
Laide Sonola & Anna Hawkes

Set & Costume Designer
Constance Villemot

Sound Designer
Sassy Watkinson

Lighting Designer
Anfy Shum

Operator
Melanie Percy

Stage Manager
Josephine Bakewell

Fight & Intimacy Director
Enric Ortuño

Development Support
Tessa Hart

*Note: This script went to print before the end of rehearsals and may vary slightly from that presented on stage.

Characters

Acorn
Clownier
Daniel
Fatima
George
Hugo
John
Karen
Maria
Phone (voice)
Patricia
Sandy
Siri (voice)
Tom
Vision of Bernadette
Voice of Bernadette

Notes

Scenes have titles, not numbers, and the play was written so it can be jumbled in different orders, and still make sense. The following order provides one set of emphases, but, not the definitive author's vision. The thematic tides of the scenes, and how these flow from one to another, are more important than a traditional arc.

Doubling

This play was written with doubling of roles in mind. But that is an ideal, not a necessity.

Dignity

CLOWNIER
I love you so much. I can't tell you how much it-

George puts his finger on Clownier's lips. They kiss.

CLOWNIER
Goodbye.

They kiss again. George cries. Clownier takes a handkerchief out of her sleeve to dry George's face. The handkerchief is connected to many other handkerchiefs, so as she pulls on them, they just keep on coming. Clownier gets to the end of the handkerchiefs and dries his tears, taking care not to smudge his make-up.

CLOWNIER
Keep smiling.

George helps Clownier up on to a chair. Facing her fate, a noose, calmly, she closes her eyes. Lights down.

I Can't Laugh

HUGO fights with Fatima, who is in a full burqa and hijab: her skin entirely covered. PATRICIA watches to the side. They start with pushing, before advancing to kicks and punches, grabbing each other in headlocks, biting, throws and grapples. Despite the duration of the fight, they never seem fatigued or injured. To end it all, Fatima draws a knife and HUGO a heavy lamp. Simultaneously FATIMA stabs HUGO in the stomach, whilst he knocks her out with the lamp. Fatima falls instantly to the floor, seemingly unconscious. HUGO stumbles about, appearing to slowly die from the knife wedged in him. He is able to pull the blade free, but in doing so, collapses, dead. After a moment of lying lifelessly, HUGO jumps to his feet with a smile.

HUGO
Thank you Fatima.

Fatima stands up instantly, dusts herself off, gives HUGO a salute, before exiting effortlessly on Heelies (a kind of embedded roller-skate within normal-looking shoes).

HUGO
Fatima's our best fight choreographer. No one takes a fake lamp to the head like Fatima. Just to give you an idea of what we could be aiming for.

PATRICIA
I think you might have me mixed up with another person?

HUGO (*Realising*)
PATRICIA, isn't it? I'm so thick sometimes: must be the hormones. Please accept my apologies, we have a young lady coming in later this afternoon who wanted some fight choreography doing. You, however... don't tell me don't tell me...

HUGO stares at PATRICIA, straining to remember all the details of her request.

HUGO
A clue might help?

PATRICIA
I'm here to train my laugh-

HUGO (*Quickly*)
Laughter training. (*Beat*) Yes yes yes. Now I remember. Sorry again. But. Then again... *free show*. Am I right? Never harms.

PATRICIA
I was told this was an all-round acting school?

HUGO
It is. Having said that... it doesn't have to be a lamp, of course. I could hit you on the head with a soap dish, or... you could aggravate my eczema with four thimbles and a thumble?

PATRICIA considers leaving.

HUGO
That was my first attempt at a joke, to get the giggle ball rolling onwards.

HUGO sucks his teeth.

HUGO (*Jovial shouting*)
Fatima you're fired!

HUGO looks to PATRICIA for a reaction she doesn't get.

HUGO (*Suddenly serious*)
So what is it about your laugh that you want to change? Too loud?

HUGO does a loud laugh.

HUGO
Too meek?

HUGO does a meek laugh.

HUGO
Too haughty?

HUGO does a haughty laugh.

HUGO
Too sexy?

HUGO does a sexy laugh.

HUGO
Not sexy enough?

HUGO does a sad, frumpy laugh.

HUGO
Is it a dirty laugh?

HUGO does a dirty laugh.

HUGO
A woodpecker chuckle?

HUGO does a Woody Woodpecker laugh.

HUGO
Do you laugh like a bag of gravel?

HUGO does a Mutley laugh.

HUGO
Is it a wispy whistler?

HUGO does a wheezy old hillbilly laugh.

HUGO
Does your laugh sound like a hippopotamus, a porn star at climax or a bit of both on a rusty see-saw?

HUGO does a monstrously over-the-top uncontrollable laugh.

HUGO
Or is it just dull?

Beat.

PATRICIA
I haven't smiled or laughed for nearly five years.

HUGO
WTB: what the Buddha? Are you serious, you are you're serious aren't you, look at you, you're so serious. (*Beat*) Not laughed, ok, but not *smiled?* (*Beat*) *Five years?!*

PATRICIA
I was looking around at different acting schools, and on your website-

HUGO
Needs updating. Sorry go on.

PATRICIA
It says on your website that you focus a lot on comic performance?

HUGO
Of course. I mean you've seen my movies?

PATRICIA
I... no I don't think / I have

HUGO (*Pretend scandalised*)
The impudence, effrontery and down right audacity of this woman! I'm kidding- but seriously you haven't seen Teddy Ninjas?

PATRICIA
I... You were in that one?

HUGO (*Pretend modesty*)
Only the marquee star darling, though I suppose as my breakout performance that one could have passed under your radar. You'll have seen the famous bakery scene on YouTube: I'm wearing nothing but a bakers hat and batting scones away with a stale cheese twist? (*Genuinely insulted*) That went viral for the best part of two years, do you live in a cave? (*Beat*) Tell me you'd at least heard of me and that formed part of your decision? (*Beat. Mumbling to himself*) Never / in all my years

PATRICIA (*Trying to be believable*)
Oh, yes of course, I mean *heard of*, yes. Yes, I'd heard of you, just not. Put a face to a name. Yet. I mean as soon as I went on the school's website-

HUGO
Needs updating. I'm like nine in the profile pics: so embarrassing. I don't even have my character mole in a single shot.

PATRICIA
Character / mole?

HUGO
See?

HUGO turns his head to reveal a dark mole on his jaw.

HUGO
My last agent thought it would add edge to my performances, get me a few meatier roles, so I had it surgically attached.

PATRICIA
Don't people usually get moles like that removed?

HUGO
Well yes, my agent. It was *her* mole. My problem is that I'm too symmetrical: golden ratio. People find it eerie, apparently. *Weirdos*. So a spot of imperfection to highlight the otherwise angelic visage. Strange though- I would swear it's

been growing if it could do such a thing. And it doesn't half get itchy.

PATRICIA
I think you should have that checked out, maybe?

Pause.

HUGO
Nothing?

PATRICIA
Nothing?

HUGO
How extraordinary. I'm not talking about my fee, which is astronomical. Nothing, as in, you didn't even flinch that whole time. Not a flitter of a smile.

PATRICIA
Oh. Were you joking, about the mole?

HUGO
Yes, I was joking. It's a sultana.

HUGO eats his "mole".

HUGO
Still nothing. Amazing. You see how far I'm willing to go for you and this laugh? I will even lie about fruit.

PATRICIA

See, I know that was meant to be funny: it's not that I can't, it's that I've stopped. It's like I've forgotten. What I was thinking is, maybe you could teach me how to fake laugh, then perhaps if I do that, I might be able to rediscover my own. Through practice, or... breathing, or, I don't know. You follow?

Beat.

HUGO
You really don't find me funny?

PATRICIA
Sorry.

HUGO
I think we should probably be friends: I often wonder if people aren't just laughing because they work for me. (*Beat*) I haven't been in a movie for two years. Of course you wouldn't know that- you haven't even heard of me.

PATRICIA
I'm really more of a / book person

HUGO
No, no. It's ok. (*Beat*) I shouldn't think of myself as an actor. I run an acting school. Or rather, my mother runs an acting school, and I prance about in between meals. I'm not famous anymore. Not really. (*Beat*) I'm probably six months away from *Celebrity Big Brother*. (*Beat*) *Ant & Dec* wouldn't even have me.

PATRICIA
Can we, actually / sorry

HUGO
You are my Everest, Patricia.

PATRICIA
That's wonderful, but I have to leave in twenty minutes for an appointment, so.

HUGO
You are my Holy Grail. When you open up to laughter, the world shall be complete - my life shall be complete.

PATRICIA
Aren't you twelve?

HUGO
Eleven and five eighths. (*Beat*) Alright, shall we get started?

Is It Christmas?

SANDY
Merry Christmas darling!

JOHN
Is it?

SANDY
Merry Christmas!

JOHN
Is it Christmas?

SANDY
Is it Christmas? Of course it's bloody Christmas, why else would you buy me all them presents?

SANDY points over to the presents.

JOHN
I did? Yes, I did, of course.

SANDY
I love you, John.

JOHN
I love you too...

JOHN tries to remember SANDY's name, but can't.

SANDY
Sandy, dear. What are you like?

SANDY kisses JOHN on the lips.

JOHN
Are we having turkey?

SANDY
Isn't Christmas day without turkey.

JOHN
Stuffing? Both kinds?

SANDY
The kind you stuff up the bird's bum and the other one too, aye-

JOHN
"Stuff up the bird's bum", what are you like?

SANDY
You put your feet up, don't worry about me.

JOHN
Hey.

JOHN fetches a present and passes it to SANDY.

SANDY
What is it?

JOHN
Open it.

SANDY opens the present. It's a lamp.

JOHN
It's a lamp.

SANDY
You know me so well, JOHN. I love it.

JOHN
You do? Oh good. What time will Mandy be coming by?

Beat.

SANDY
She rang to say she'll be a bit late. Hey. Give me a kiss.

JOHN kisses SANDY.

SANDY
You can do better than that!

JOHN and SANDY kiss for a long time.

JOHN
If I was ten years younger...

SANDY laughs and playfully pats JOHN on the arm.

First draft

DANIEL addresses the audience, sometimes checking lines on an iPad he has in his hand. His speech is flat and without charisma, but not unconfident.

DANIEL

Unhappiness of employees costs the US economy $500 billion a year in lost productivity, lost tax receipts and health-care costs. $500 billion a year. (*Beat*) The internet: perhaps the greatest invention known to man. The cloud. Your knowledge is his, his is yours. Boundaries are gone. A child in Africa can read about... whatever he wants. The world is our oyster. (*Beat*) Cancer. Every day laboratories step closer towards curing the world's worst diseases. AIDs. HIV. (*Beat*) Air travel. Yesterday I was in London, today with you in Abu Dhabi, tomorrow Tokyo.

DANIEL walks about thinking, before returning to his speech.

DANIEL
We are entering an age where living to 200 is not an unfeasible idea. It isn't science fiction. It's science fact. But even with all our medical, economic and scientific advances, the biggest taboo of them all holds us back. How we live. Who we are. Why we get up in the morning. Happiness.

DANIEL is unhappy. He talks to his iPad.

DANIEL
Siri?

Siri
Hello Daniel.

DANIEL
Is my speech an embarrassment?

Siri
Would you like me to find examples of famous speeches?

DANIEL
No. Thank you Siri.

Siri
No problem.

Beat. DANIEL reads his speech back to himself.

DANIEL (*To himself, quietly*)
But even with all our medical... the biggest taboo... why we get up... (*Louder, to the audience*) Different levels of emotion

are inscribed and visible in the brain. For years, the technology has existed to translate different emotional responses into visualised data: objective data. Our governments have invested trillions of dollars into assessing the impact of different behaviours upon the human mind and body, through social indexes, medical trials, all without seeing the bigger picture. Our mood is a measurement of chemicals, we knew this, but now we can use it, we *are* using it. We are told throughout our lives that to be satisfied with ourselves is the hardest thing: as soon as you know you've got it good, it slips away. Well today, with the launch of the EmotiPiece, I say happiness is no longer the ghost in the machine.

DANIEL holds up his wrist, on which is an experimental watch, The EmotiPiece.

DANIEL
Happiness *is* the machine, which will drive our economy forward into a new golden age, where the human species is optimized to reach his full potential. Thank you. (*Beat. To himself, quietly*) Round of applause, bags of cash, beautiful women. (*Beat*) Fuck.

No Steve Jobs

    DANIEL *slouches in a chair, watching a speech by Steve Jobs on his iPad. The audio can be heard. Jobs makes a joke. The audience in the video laughs. DANIEL squirms.*

    DANIEL (*Sarcastic*)
Everybody loves Steve. Steve was the greatest.

    DANIEL *pauses the video, considers his life. He presses a button on his watch. There is a release of compressed air, and DANIEL's mood is lifted. He sits up.*

    DANIEL
SIRI.

    SIRI
Hello Daniel.

    DANIEL
How can I be a better person?

SIRI
Would you like me to find online self-help forums?

Beat.

DANIEL
No... no. (*Beat*) Siri.

SIRI
Yes Daniel? (*Beat*) Can I help / you?

DANIEL
Yes. Yes to the self-help. I want. Find me videos: a Ted Talk, or something. About... being...

Beat.

SIRI
Would you like me to find Ted Talk videos on the nature of existence?

DANIEL
No I wasn't. I hadn't finished my... Yeah ok. The brain.

SIRI
Would you like to see *your* Ted Talk?

DANIEL
No fucking way. Oh. Bernadette... what's her name? Big boobs. Psychologist.

SIRI
Would you like me to search for videos with big boobs?

DANIEL
No. *(Beat)* Well... *(Beat)* Search for videos of a psychologist called Bernadette something-something. She gave a speech at the World Economic Forum last year.

SIRI
I have found 132 videos of Bernadette Coleman-Morris-

DANIEL
That's the! Yes.

DANIEL taps through the results.

DANIEL *(Gleefully)*
Yesss...

We Are Creating the Problem

DANIEL sits on a chair masturbating, holding his iPad with the other hand. A vision of Bernadette stands in front of him, swaying her hips and accentuating her curves. Occasionally DANIEL looks down at the iPad to fix the image of Bernadette in his mind, before closing his eyes again. Her voice is separate to her body.

VOICE OF BERNADETTE
I am very happy –yes, happy– to be invited to speak here, not because I feel particularly at home, but because this is an opportunity for me to talk to you directly. For years I have read about this Forum with a certain level of disgust at the terminology being banded about. We, by which I mean *you*, talk about the mental wellbeing of employees as the key to productivity. But do you not see? You are creating the problem you are trying to solve. The capitalist system quite simply excludes the-

Boos from the audience.

VOICE OF BERNADETTE
Excludes and alienates the individual: her emotions, her dreams, her individuality.

The boos grow louder. DANIEL stops masturbating and looks at his iPad.

VOICE OF BERNADETTE
This word "Happiness" has just become another tool for the exploitation of workers, for private profit.

DANIEL clicks on another video.

VOICE OF BERNADETTE
Yes Slavoj, I accept your critique. I am 100% on the same page as you.

DANIEL puts the iPad down and starts to masturbate with his eyes closed again. The vision of Bernadette sways.

VOICE OF BERNADETTE
Of course, to dismantle the systems of surveillance now ubiquitous in our Western so-called democracies-

The VOICE OF BERNADETTE nose-laughs for a time at her own cynicisms. DANIEL picks his iPad up and clicks on the video: making the sound of her nose-laugh repeat on loop he masturbates furiously. After losing energy he lets the video roll. Though his hand is still down his trousers, it is more out of absent-mindedness. DANIEL watches the video earnestly.

VOICE OF BERNADETTE
To dismantle these systems would result in a reduction of the relative happiness, health and wealth of the populous: note how I use the word *relative* here, because what I am saying is that the terms of the argument are wrong; we've got it all wrong. Who we are. How we live.

KAREN, an employee, walks in. She is instantly horrified by the sight of DANIEL with his hand down his trousers.

KAREN
Sorry-

Exit KAREN.

The vision of BERNADETTE disappears. DANIEL stands up. He considers what to do.

DANIEL (*Shouting*)
Michelle? Michelle?

Enter KAREN. She averts her eyes.

DANIEL
Michelle. I want a coffee. Strong, black, two sugars.

KAREN sighs.

KAREN
My name is Karen.

KAREN turns away.

DANIEL
Hey.

KAREN turns to look at DANIEL with barely hidden hatred.

DANIEL
You should smile more.

She exits in a huff.

KAREN
This never happened at Apple!

Beat. DANIEL looks like a small lost child. He presses the button on his watch. There is a release of compressed air.

Lady Lunch

MARIA
Mr. Daniel. I didn't know you were in the country.

DANIEL
Had some time before Hong Kong and needed to... I told my wife I was on my way, is she not... about?

MARIA
No sir. Would you like something to eat, Mr. Daniel-

DANIEL
Did she leave you any messages? Or...

MARIA sees DANIEL wants some hope, something she can't give. She smiles with tight lips- DANIEL sighs. MARIA starts to give DANIEL a shoulder rub.

MARIA
Feel good?

DANIEL squirms.

DANIEL
Did she say when she'd be back?

MARIA
Mrs. Charlotte? She's at one of her lady lunches.

DANIEL
Don't call it a "lady lunch", Maria. You make it sound like they're lesbians, eating each other out. It's much more medicated and drab than that.

DANIEL takes MARIA's hand and moves it to the knot in his neck. MARIA continues.

DANIEL
How has the house been without me?

MARIA
Master Thomas has missed you.

DANIEL
Higher.

MARIA
Here?

MARIA adjusts the massage position.

MARIA
I haven't been to my house in a month. Actually it's been pretty tiring?

MARIA massages deeply- DANIEL's face screws up, somewhere between pleasure and pain.

MARIA
My friend's birthday tonight.

DANIEL's hand touches the inside of MARIA's thigh.

MARIA
She invited me for drinks but I didn't think I could go.

MARIA pauses her massage, but doesn't stop DANIEL reaching up her leg.

MARIA
Mr. Daniel...

DANIEL
How many times MARIA- it's just *DANIEL*, please.

MARIA turns to face DANIEL.

MARIA
Maybe I can go now you are here?

DANIEL touches MARIA's face.

DANIEL
I think I need you.

DANIEL pulls MARIA close and they start to have sex. Enter Tom. He freezes, in shock. MARIA sees him.

MARIA
Master Thomas!

Exit Tom.

DANIEL
Fuck.

Walking On Sunshine

CLOWNIER sings 'Walking On Sunshine' by Katrina & the Waves whilst juggling four bananas. Her performance is just on the competent side of lacklustre.

TOM
Are you a girl?

CLOWNIER throws the bananas high, and lets them fall down her top. She shakes her arms so a banana pops out of each sleeve. She points the bananas at TOM like she is a cowboy.

TOM
I could have done that.

CLOWNIER peels and eats the bananas.

CLOWNIER
You didn't though, did you?

CLOWNIER chucks the skins on the floor.

TOM
My mom is going to be pissed.

CLOWNIER shakes her arms again: no bananas come out. She shakes her right leg: no bananas come out. She shakes her left leg: two bananas come out. She picks them up, unpeels and eats them, throwing the skins on the floor near the other two.

TOM
Are you deaf?

CLOWNIER shakes her left leg again. One more banana falls out.

TOM
I said, *are you deaf?*

CLOWNIER shakes her left leg for ages, and three, four bananas fall out.

CLOWNIER
Yes.

CLOWNIER quickly unpeels and eats them all, creating a circle on the floor out of the discarded skins.

TOM
Girls aren't funny.

CLOWNIER takes a run-up to the down-turned skins.

TOM
Don't bother.

CLOWNIER stops still.

CLOWNIER
When I said I take tips...

TOM
My mom paid for a boy clown.

CLOWNIER
Look kid, it really shouldn't matter.

TOM
Actually, I'm a Muslim, so yes it does.

CLOWNIER
No you're not.

TOM
How dare you insult my faith.

CLOWNIER
I literally just saw you eat twelve ham vol-au-vents.

TOM
I thought clowns were meant to be funny?

CLOWNIER
I thought birthday parties were meant to have friends.

Beat. TOM looks like he is going to explode.

CLOWNIER
Look, sorry- I'm not enjoying this anymore than you are.

TOM
You're fired, ok! You're fired! (*Quieter*) You're fired...

CLOWNIER
Come on now, don't-

TOM
They couldn't come, ok? All my friends were busy today.

Beat. TOM wipes his eyes repeatedly.

CLOWNIER
Ok.

TOM
I want you to fuck off now.

CLOWNIER
I could just tell your mum that you're being a brat.

TOM
Who's she gonna believe?

Beat.

CLOWNIER
Guess I'll just sit here until 3 o'clock then.

CLOWNIER sits. TOM hasn't got a solution. CLOWNIER's silence is torture to him.

TOM starts crying again.

CLOWNIER
You know your mom or dad should have realised I was a woman when they booked me. I mean it's pretty obvious. (*Beat*) Clownier Schiffer?

CLOWNIER pulls one handkerchief partially from her sleeve, and tries to dry his face. TOM pulls away.

TOM
I'm not- (*Sniffles*) Crying.

TOM turns his back, and stands facing away from her, letting the tears fall untouched.

CLOWNIER
Look, let's start again, ok? It's *your* birthday. We could... talk? Instead. If you like.

TOM snorts up some snot.

TOM
I'm not crying.

CLOWNIER
Ok? Ok.

CLOWNIER gets herself together.

CLOWNIER
Your mom will want to know why I'm leaving. She's paying me for two hours.

TOM turns to face CLOWNIER.

TOM
If you show me your tits, you can stay.

CLOWNIER
I beg your... what did / you

TOM
Show me your tits, and you can stay.

Beat.

CLOWNIER
Wow. (*Beat*) I'll show myself out-

TOM
Don't... (*Beat*) Please don't tell my mom.

CLOWNIER
About the crying or the misogyny?

TOM
Just... *could* we start again, actually? Please. I want us to start again.

Beat. TOM realises that CLOWNIER has made her mind up.

TOM takes off his EmotiPiece watch and holds it out to CLOWNIER.

TOM
Take the watch.

CLOWNIER
What? No.

TOM
Take the watch.

CLOWNIER
I'm not taking your watch.

TOM
Take it you bitch, you know you need it: look at you. It's probably worth more money than you've ever seen in your life. Take it. Take it and fuck off.

Beat.

CLOWNIER
Has being stupidly rich made you happy, Tom? Has getting every material thing you have ever wanted, when you wanted, made you happy?

TOM
Yes.

Beat.

CLOWNIER
Good answer.

CLOWNIER turns to leave.

TOM
Slut.

Exit CLOWNIER.

TOM
I bet these don't even-

TOM stands on one of the banana skins. He slips over and hits the floor hard, knocking himself out.

Your Call is Important to Us

GEORGE has his mobile on speakerphone.

PHONE
Thank you for calling the emergency services. To ensure your call is connected to the correct department, please listen to the following options. For police, press one. (*Long beat*) For ambulance, press-

GEORGE presses 2. There is a long silence.

PHONE
Your call is important to us. Please hold.

An elevator-music style cover of 'Walking on Sunshine' plays. GEORGE stays sat, waiting.

Smile From the Ears

HUGO
To smile is in the face. Not just the muscles around the mouth, but the eyes too. If your eyes aren't smiling, your nose, then what we as the receiver of the smile get is a broken image. Try a smile for me now.

PATRICIA smiles.

HUGO
Ok, ok... Great, thank you.

PATRICIA
Was that great?

HUGO
It was awful, honey. You looked like you'd just smelt something, and you were trying to work out if it was good cheese or bad meat. What I'd like you to try for me, is to smile from the ears. Got it?

PATRICIA
How do you even...

PATRICIA concentrates on trying to achieve "smiling from her ears".

HUGO
Am I speaking Esperanto here? *From* the ears. Your ears. What are you...

PATRICIA tries her best, but absolutely cannot achieve the task.

PATRICIA
That was it, wasn't it? (*Beat*) No? I have it: look.

PATRICIA smiles unconvincingly.

HUGO
Patricia darling. You certainly have *something*. It may be Parkinson's, or the remnants of a stroke... Forget the ears, just-

PATRICIA
Is this it?

PATRICIA smiles a different, weird smile.

HUGO
Patricia, please stop before you die, or I die, or I want to die. No more ears, in fact no more smiling. I need a vape: ten-minute comfort breakio.

PATRICIA
But we've only just / started

HUGO (*Loud and aggressive*)
Comfort breakio!!

Lights down.

A Broken Image

Lights up. PATRICIA is smiling, showing her teeth. She gestures to HUGO to get his approval. In reply, HUGO does his own smile, demonstrating good practice. PATRICIA relaxes her face before trying a new smile. HUGO gives her the "so-so" gesture, before micromanaging her grin with pokes and tweaks.

HUGO
Yes! Don't. Move. I'm fetching you a mirror.

Exit HUGO. PATRICIA tries to fix her expression. A fly enters the space and starts to bother her. She tries to ignore it, then has to shoo it out of the space, all whilst keeping the smile. The fly leaves.

Enter HUGO with a mirror. As he approaches her, he loses the bounce in his step, horrified at what he sees on PATRICIA's face.

HUGO
What the fuck have you done?

PATRICIA (*Without moving her lips*)
There was a fly.

PATRICIA breaks the smile and rubs her face.

PATRICIA
I think I pulled my chin.

Lights down.

Never Undermine a Montage

Lights up.

HUGO
Ok, now... shoot!

PATRICIA smiles quickly at HUGO, like a gunshot.

HUGO (*In raptures*)
Yes! Again!

PATRICIA smiles again.

HUGO
And *hooooold...*

PATRICIA holds the smile.

HUGO
And... relax! By the cheeks of McCauley the Beautiful, I think we have it!

HUGO holds his hand up for a high five. PATRICIA doesn't reciprocate.

HUGO
Don't you dare leave me hanging you bitch.

HUGO taps the underside of PATRICIA's hands with his high five.

PATRICIA
I just. I don't know Hugo, I just-

HUGO
Don't. Don't you dare jinx this and undermine the montage. Never undermine a montage.

PATRICIA
I know what I'm doing *looks* like a smile. I just...

HUGO
Don't feel it? Inside?

PATRICIA
It just feels like I'm stretching my mouth.

HUGO
That's where stage two comes begins.

PATRICIA
Stage two?

HUGO
Patricia. We're gonna find your laugh.

The EmotiPiece

DANIEL
I got you something. (*Beat*) I said I got you something. Thomas.

DANIEL tries to turn TOM's head to face him. TOM turns sharply away from DANIEL.

DANIEL
Look at your father when he's talking to you.

TOM faces DANIEL. The stare of confused anger makes DANIEL squirm. DANIEL offers out the present to TOM. He doesn't take it.

TOM
It was my birthday *last* week.

DANIEL screws his face up in realisation.

DANIEL
I... *knew* that, which is why I got you this.

DANIEL holds out the box with a big, plastic smile.

TOM
Do you love her?

Pause.

DANIEL
Of course I don't love Maria-

TOM
Mom! Do you love mom?

DANIEL
It was just sex, Thomas. You'll understand when you're older.

TOM grabs the box from DANIEL without breaking eye contact- DANIEL doesn't let go, and they both grip on it. TOM starts to dig his fingers into the box.

DANIEL
Stop, you're gonna damage it-

DANIEL pulls the box out of TOM's grip. He takes the watch out of the box and puts it on TOM's wrist.

DANIEL
This is more than a watch- it's a prototype EmotiPiece. It measures the endorphin levels in your body constantly. Inside there's a capsule and compressed air and what it

does is release... it's called Oxytocin, these chemicals into your blood stream, to top up your positivity. I've also got replacement cartridges. No one else has one of these, so it's top-secret stuff. Can I get a James Bond secret five?

DANIEL turns his back and sticks his hand out behind him to receive a low-five. TOM doesn't reciprocate.

DANIEL
Ok, I have to run- I have a plane to catch. Be good for Maria, alright? Oh- and you'll need the user guide for that. WhatsApp me to remind me and I'll forward it to you. Will you remember to do that? It's important not to press it too much, ok? Ok? (*Beat*) You know I love your mom, DANIEL. You do know that, don't you?

TOM
I don't need a nanny anymore.

DANIEL
I'm not sure if that's-

TOM
Or I tell mom.

Pause.

DANIEL
Reality check, TOM. Your mom has been fucking around my back for years.

TOM is dumbstruck.

DANIEL
It's fine. Everything... is fine.

TOM hugs DANIEL tightly.

DANIEL
Hey, hey. None of that.

DANIEL pulls out of the hug and offers a handshake instead.

DANIEL
Man of the house.

TOM doesn't let go of DANIEL's hand- gripping tightly. DANIEL is confused.

TOM
How old am I?

DANIEL
I would have been here if I could have been- you know that. Next birthday, I promise-

TOM
It's my birthday TOMorrow.

DANIEL closes his eyes, sighing with a mixture of shame and apathy.

DANIEL
You don't need me at your party. I'll just embarrass you in front of your friends.

TOM lets go of his dad's hand.

DANIEL
I'll sack Maria. Ok? No nanny.

TOM starts to cry.

DANIEL
Hey now. Stop crying- your mom doesn't need that. (*Beat*) Happy Birthday big man.

TOM looks at his new EmotiPiece.

I... Don't Know

SANDY
Merry Christmas John!

JOHN
Is it?

SANDY
Merry Christmas!

JOHN
Is it Christmas?

SANDY
Is it...? Of course it's bloody... why else would you buy me all them presents?

SANDY points over to the presents.

JOHN
I did? Yes, I did, of course.

SANDY
I love you, John.

JOHN
I love you too...

JOHN tries to remember SANDY's name, but can't.

SANDY
Sandy, dear. I'm Sandy.

Beat.

JOHN
Yes I know that.

SANDY
What are you like?

SANDY kisses JOHN on the lips.

JOHN
Are we having turkey?

SANDY
Isn't Christmas day without turkey.

JOHN
Stuffing? Both kinds?

SANDY
The kind you stuff up the bird's bum and the other kind too, aye. (*Long beat*) You put your feet up, don't worry about me.

JOHN stands in a dumb state. SANDY can't help but stare. Beat.

JOHN
Hey.

JOHN fetches a present and passes it to SANDY.

SANDY
What is it?

Beat.

JOHN
I... don't know.

SANDY opens the present. It's the same lamp from before.

SANDY
What is it?

JOHN
It's...

JOHN studies the object hard. He cannot process what it is. SANDY watches him closely.

SANDY (*Defeated*)
What a beautiful lamp.

JOHN
A lamp, yes, of course.

SANDY
You know me so well, JOHN. I love it.

JOHN
You do? Oh good. What time will Mandy be coming by?

Beat.

SANDY
She rang to say she'll be a bit late. Hey. Give me a kiss.

JOHN kisses SANDY.

SANDY
You can do better than that!

JOHN and SANDY kiss for a long time.

JOHN
If I was ten years younger…

SANDY laughs and playfully pats JOHN on the arm.

Remember a Time You Felt Safe

HUGO alone on stage, instructing the audience.

HUGO
Laugh as you hum, mouth closed. Play with the pitch, up and down the scale, feeling the vibrations resonate through your body. You feel that? Now try and move it through your chest, the resonance, into your jaw, your nose, your sinus cavities, your forehead, the top of your head... now back down again. Breathe in deeply, ok out. Now this time, when you breathe out, do it in quick bursts of air, and with the last ones I want you to make a sound, to start with "ah", with those last few breaths. So you build towards those sounds, like this.

HUGO demonstrates.

HUGO

Now you. (*Beat*) Ok, now the same thing, but the sound is "ee". (*Beat*) Now "eye". (*Beat*) Now "oh". (*Beat*) Lastly "ooh". (*Beat*) Make an elongated "aeeee" sound as you slowly lift your arms all the way up. Don't take your neighbour's eyes out: I can attest to how much that stings. With your arms pointing to the sky I want you to laugh from the heart. Imagine your laugh is coming from your heart. (*Beat*) Try short laughs, loud laughs, titters, chuckles, cackles and snorts. (*Beat*) Try and remember a time when you felt safe, surrounded by people you loved, when you were truly happy. Take time to connect with that memory, laughing now as you did then.

Something Almost Happened

GEORGE, sat waiting for the call centre to answer. The music pauses, as if something is about to happen, before continuing as before.

Have a Heart

SANDY is wrapping the lamp in paper. There is a knock at the door. SANDY listens out. The knock becomes a banging. Lights down. Lights up.

PATRICIA, is stood before SANDY with an iPad in hand.

SANDY
I'll call the police.

PATRICIA
Let's keep this civil, shall we? I'm here for the money, Sandy.

SANDY
You work for Reg?

PATRICIA
Reg owed us, so he paid off his debts with a few of his customers.

SANDY
But I'm up-to-date.

PATRICIA
New management. We don't accept staggered payments anymore. The total amount is due now. If you can't pay, we'll have to come to an alternative arrangement.

SANDY
Well of course I can't pay, I don't have 20 grand lying about! If I did / I'd have paid it

PATRICIA
Alright, alright, calm down. We're not monsters. We understand you won't have that cash in the house-

SANDY
I just don't have that kind of-

PATRICIA
Just. If you can't pay-

SANDY
I-

PATRICIA
We will acquisition properties / equal to that value

SANDY
Acquisition? I don't have nothing, I don't / have nothing!

PATRICIA
SANDY, please.

SANDY
You don't know me.

PATRICIA
You knew when you took that loan what kind of man Reg was.

SANDY
I've known Reg for fifteen year, and he's always been fair to everyone what's borrowed money. We always pay him back. *I* always pay him back, I was *going* to pay / Reg back

PATRICIA
Sandy- *Mrs. Tunnock*: Reg doesn't own your debt anymore. (*Beat*) It's our debt, and the terms have changed. Now if you could point me in the direction of your TVs, iPads, washer-driers, your computer-

SANDY
I don't. I don't have any of that.

PATRICIA
Everybody has a computer. (*Beat*) Have some self-respect.

SANDY
I sold it. I don't have nothing.

PATRICIA walks about, inspecting the room.

PATRICIA
Christmas decorations in July? It's alright for some...

SANDY
Please don't take my house. Have a heart.

PATRICIA
I don't get any pleasure out of this, Sandy, I promise you.

SANDY
Have a heart. Have a heart. Please. Please.

Enter JOHN. He stands still, confused.

SANDY
Please.

JOHN walks closer to PATRICIA. He circles her, looking her up and down.

PATRICIA (*To SANDY*)
Is he...

Now JOHN is confused by who SANDY is.

JOHN
Who are you?

SANDY
It's Sandy, love.

JOHN
Well yes, obviously. Who's *that?*

JOHN points to PATRICIA.

SANDY
It's nobody.

PATRICIA
Don't think I'll not come back.

PATRICIA goes to leave.

SANDY (*To PATRICIA*)
Just, please.

PATRICIA stops in her footsteps.

SANDY
John- can you check the turkey's doing alright, I think I heard a beep.

PATRICIA
I'll be back at four. You have two hours to organise yourself.

JOHN
Are we having turkey?

SANDY
Isn't Christmas day without turkey.

JOHN
Is it Christmas?

PATRICIA
Did you hear me? I'll be bringing removal staff, so I suggest being ready.

SANDY
Just go and have a check it's not burning would you? (*Beat*) John?

JOHN
What?

SANDY
Can you go check the turkey's not burning?

JOHN
What turkey? Are we having turkey?

SANDY
Can you go to the kitchen please and check the oven!

JOHN
Alright. I'm not bloody deaf. You want your hearing checked.

Exit JOHN. SANDY slowly walks over to the lamp, lying in the open wrapping paper on the floor.

PATRICIA
What if I gave you a week?

SANDY picks the lamp up and turns it in her hand, inspecting it.

PATRICIA
Would one week help? You could speak to relatives about somewhere to stay.

SANDY
There's nobody.

PATRICIA
I'm not enjoying this anymore than you are.

SANDY
I don't have anyone.

SANDY smashes the lamp over PATRICIA's head, knocking her out.

Mandy Comes to Dinner

PATRICIA is sat at the dinner table, bound up and gagged as a hostage. SANDY watches her. PATRICIA wakes up and panics, but can't move much.

SANDY

Your name is Mandy. You're our only daughter. You live in Preston with your husband, Malcolm. You make pots, and vases, and other things out of earth, with shells you push in for decoration. You always said you wanted to be an artist, and even through your drug problems, you always made me and your father a present every year. No matter what else was happening, you always made us something, right up til the end. This year you've made us a lamp. You're the best thing me and your father have ever done, and we love you so much we've always let you get away with anything, ever since you were little. You used to be a chubby child, always demanding chocolates and sweets, and we gave em to you. Cos we love you so much and can't see you unhappy. It hurts us so much to see what you do to yourself sometimes, but even through all your problems, even all the terrible things, you're still our baby girl, and always will be. You know you've got a charmed life, but you're never shy to ask for money. You're 28. You don't have any kids. You don't love your husband. It's Christmas day.

Enter JOHN. SANDY removes PATRICIA's gag.

SANDY
Merry Christmas darling!

JOHN
Is it?

SANDY
Merry Christmas!

JOHN
Is it Christmas?

SANDY
Is it Christmas? Of course it's bloody Christmas, why else would our Mandy be here?

SANDY points over to Mandy.

JOHN
Mandy?

SANDY
It's Mandy, love. Our baby girl.

JOHN
Mandy?

SANDY (*To PATRICIA*)
Aren't you gonna say Merry Christmas to your father? Came especially for Christmas dinner, didn't you? Didn't you?

Beat.

PATRICIA
Merry Christmas, dad.

JOHN
Who are you?

SANDY
Mandy brought us a present, darling, look.

SANDY passes the wrapped lamp to JOHN.

JOHN
What?

SANDY
Mandy brought us a present.

JOHN
Did she? Thank you love.

JOHN leans in and kisses PATRICIA on the cheek.

SANDY
Open it.

JOHN opens the present.

JOHN
It's a...

JOHN can't recall what it is.

PATRICIA
I made it.

JOHN
A lamp. It's lovely dear. Have you seen this SANDY?

SANDY
Yes, JOHN. Isn't it beautiful?

JOHN
We can put it with the other ones.

SANDY
The other... whats?

JOHN
The other pots and things Mandy's made us. There's that nobbly ashtray, those egg cups you said look like testicles- sorry Mandy, your mother's words, not mine.

SANDY is eaten up by emotion.

JOHN
Don't tell me you've chucked them?

SANDY
They're safe.

JOHN
Well, good.

JOHN stands dumbly.

SANDY
I love you, John.

JOHN
I love you too...

JOHN tries to remember SANDY's name, but can't.

SANDY
SANDY, dear. What are you like?

SANDY kisses JOHN on the lips.

JOHN
Are we having turkey?

SANDY
Isn't Christmas day without turkey.

JOHN
Stuffing? Both kinds?

SANDY
The kind you stuff up the bird's bum and the other kind too, aye-

JOHN
"Stuff up the bird's bum", what are you like?

SANDY
You put your feet up, don't worry about me.

SANDY takes the lamp from JOHN's hands.

JOHN
What time will Mandy be coming by?

SANDY
Mandy's right there, John! She's right in front of you.

JOHN
That's not Mandy.

SANDY
Who else would it be?

PATRICIA
Malcolm says hello.

JOHN
Malcolm? What's she talking about?

SANDY
Malcolm's Mandy's husband, remember?

JOHN
Mandy's ten years old, Sandy, what are you like?

JOHN stands without expression.

SANDY
John- can you check the knives are sharp for the turkey?

JOHN
Are we having turkey?

SANDY
Isn't Christmas day without turkey.

JOHN
Is it Christmas?

SANDY
Of course it's bloody Christmas, what are you like? (*Long beat*) Hey. Gimme a kiss.

JOHN kisses SANDY.

SANDY
You can do better than that!

JOHN and SANDY kiss for a long time.

JOHN
If I was ten years younger...

SANDY laughs and playfully pats JOHN on the arm. He stands dumbly.

SANDY
John. The knives.

PATRICIA
Please. Please.

Clownier Is Upset

CLOWNIER cries uncontrollably.

I'm Underneath

MARIA

Hello, my name is Maria. I'm 32. I'm originally from Colombia, but now living in London, looking for work, and a good time with guys who are a bit crazy like me. I like fucking. A lot. I'm not a shy person, as you can see, I know what I want and I go for it. I am looking for a man who also is not scared of life, who is passionate about his job, his interests. Who is interested in foreign women, maybe, a bit of different culture. I say this because I know some guys they get scared of me because I go for it, everything. I've dated Americans in the past, I lived in the US, but never a British man, but I know you guys have the reputation of being quiet, or shy. I'm a big character, and I need attention. So if you are ready for big arguments *and* lots of hot fucking, then message me. I will do anything. I've tried almost everything at least once, so I don't have boundaries. All you have to do is ask. Also, I am carrying a bit of extra weight at the moment, but I'm on a gluten-free diet which I started yesterday, which is driving me mad, so. Be patient. This isn't me: I'm underneath. Ok, peace and love, send me a message. Adios.

Who You Are and What You Do

HUGO
Force a laugh.

PATRICIA
But there's so much sadness.

HUGO
Famine, war, yes. But try and forget that.

PATRICIA
The more I try not to think about it...

HUGO
Ok, well think about yourself, then. Your job, for example. Try and laugh at what you do, a funny person you met, an annoying person.

PATRICIA
My job isn't funny.

HUGO
Even if you don't find it particularly funny, make yourself laugh.

PATRICIA
I really don't think I / can

HUGO
Ok ok, Patricia. Listen, girl. Laughing at something doesn't mean it isn't serious.

PATRICIA
I evict people from their houses. I reclaim their cars. Destroy their livelihood.

HUGO
There's what you've done, ok... your experiences, your job and relationships, that's over here...

HUGO gestures to one side.

HUGO
Let's look at all of that, from a bit back. Globally. *Celestially.* (*Beat*) That means from the stars, right?

PATRICIA
I don't understand how this will help with making me laugh.

HUGO
Ok, listen. Showbiz is full of people eaten up by missed opportunities. "What if I had spoken to that casting director at the party?" "What if I didn't have a perfect golden ratio bone structure that some people apparently find eerie?". The shit that happens to us, and the shit we have done to other people... it isn't you. You are something else,

PATRICIA
It still happened, though.

HUGO
Hit yourself.

PATRICIA
Hit?

HUGO hits himself in the face and really hurts his eye. He turns away, shielding his eye.

PATRICIA
Are you-

HUGO (*Containing rage*)
I'm fine, just...

PATRICIA
I might not do / that one

HUGO (*Release of anger*)
Fuck! I got the nail right on... the dark bit of the eye, the-

PATRICIA
Pupil?

HUGO
Is it pink?

HUGO turns to show PATRICIA his hurt eye.

No Timewasters

MARIA

Hello, I'm Maria, I'm 32 and I'm Colombian, living and working in London. Looking for a good time with a guy who isn't shy, who like to have fun, but also not an asshole, ok? No assholes, please. No wideboys, no funboys, no wannabe Corleones. I'm a big personality, but I'm not invincible, ok? I'm not T2000, my skin it bleeds blood, alright? I like sex, but a bit of conversation sometimes is nice as well. Hygiene and conversation. I like a man who takes care over himself, I don't ask for much. I just want someone to bite into, someone to laugh with. You can pull my hair and ride me: that's all cool. I've taken a few spankings in my life, so if you like being tied up, or tying me up, that's cool, and if you're not, then get ready. Be ready to explore yourself because I'm a mad scientist in the bedroom. But the bedroom, that is second to respect. I don't want nobody who doesn't respect himself, who doesn't love his mother. I want somebody with a big heart, like mine, who wants to grab every day by the horns and really fucking do it. Sad guys, guys down on everything... shoo. Don't even bother. I want to laugh, to sing, and to be fucked like I'm 15. I'm on a no lacto diet, so all this extra, it's going, ok? But maybe you like to grab it? Give me a message. No timewasters. Adios.

Tap-dancing

GEORGE tap-dances slowly to the hold music.

Revealing the You That's Hidden

HUGO
Maybe we're looking at this the wrong way. We're trying to cure a broken leg with a kiss from daddy and a lollypop. You say the last time you laughed was five years ago? So I'm guessing you remember the last time you *did* laugh, or maybe... maybe the reason why you stopped?

PATRICIA
Oh, yeah, I know why I stopped laughing.

HUGO (*Relieved*)
Ok, fantastic! Great! Maybe that's our way in. So what happened?

PATRICIA
I got attacked.

HUGO (*Shocked*)
What?

PATRICIA
I got... sexually, attacked- assaulted. In the park. Five years ago in August. Since then... I just haven't found myself able to... *laugh*. (*Beat*) They say laughter and reaching orgasm is the same mechanism, don't they? I read that somewhere. It's a release of your inside, of your inside you. Revealing the you that's hidden. I've not been with anyone either, in that time. I've not had sex, climaxed.

Beat.

HUGO
Patricia. I can't help you my love. You need to speak to someone qualified. (*Beat*) I've not even had a girlfriend for longer than a week, and even that was just to promote a brand of biscuit. (*Beat*) That was all really inappropriate information to share with a child, you know that?

PATRICIA
Sorry.

HUGO
Seriously, get help.

Clownier is Numb, Patricia is Trying

CLOWNIER stands completely still, numb to the world. Alongside this, PATRICIA goes through different smiles. She exercises her muscles, rubbing her face with her hands, trying to provoke a natural grin. The smiles she produces are false, scary almost.

Someone Who's Real

MARIA

Ok, I'm Maria, I'm 33. I come from Colombia. I've lived in the UK for like a year now. I lost my virginity when I was 12 to a guy who was like a few years older- I know that sounds fucked up, but the village I'm from it isn't so weird. I like to tell people this now, because some guys get freaked out by my past, like I should be more "normal", or "more like other girls" they know, or whatever. Well I'm not other girls. I'm me. This is me, here, ok? Have a look. If you don't like it, don't contact me. Don't think you gonna save me, or change me. I'm a grown person, and I know what I like and I know what I don't fucking like, ok? If you want me to be impressed... one: be nice to me. Nasty guys, guys who think they're tough, or think that girls want mean guys? Fuck off, ok. I don't need that shit. I have fucked plenty of guys who just want one thing, and maybe that was fine then, but now I'm older, and I'm tired, ok? So be fucking nice, ok? Be a real person. I am real. I know I've got a fat ass, big legs. I have cellulites. Don't tell me I need to lose weight, don't wish I wasn't this size, cos I've fucking tried everything: I've done palleo, I've done raw, I've done only fruits, I've done shakes. This is me, ok? But don't think I'm one of those sad fat bitches you know who'll take any piece of shit. If you a prude, or if you wanna just fuck, don't message me. Right now I just need someone who's real. I'll do most things if you ask me nicely, but, really, what I want is to laugh. I love jokes, funny movies, and I'm funny too, a bit crazy, so if you get scared by a woman who bites back, then walk away. I'm curious. I want you to be curious as well. Message me if you tick these boxes, if not... don't even think about it. Adios.

More than this

PATRICIA's flat. There is no furniture, just a couple of pillows on the floor with a single sheet. PATRICIA is sat, MARIA stood.

MARIA
When you said you had an apartment here, I thought wowww... I can't wait to see the décor: I bet she has really nice curtains, expensive carpet, designer sofa. Don't get me wrong, it's nice, but...Where the fuck is your furniture? You a Buddhist junior Marie Kondo, or just spend all you make on rent?

PATRICIA
Don't need to be shy.

MARIA
I'm not shy.

PATRICIA
Come and sit with me, then.

MARIA
I only squat on the floor when I'm drunk or taking a shit, so I suggest you find me some alcohol.

PATRICIA
Red wine?

MARIA
I don't like wine.

PATRICIA
That's all I have.

MARIA retrieves a tiny bottle of vodka from between her breasts.

MARIA
Emergency supply. This is the only one I have on me. I don't stick a gin in my ass, or a rum in the... You don't smile easily, do you? Most guys laugh when I take it out. The bottle.

PATRICIA
You go for guys normally?

MARIA
Normally, yeah, sure.

PATRICIA
You seem... shy, or / nervous

MARIA
Hey, I'm not nervous, or fucking shy, ok?

PATRICIA
Sorry... You said you were curious on your profile.

MARIA
I am. But just cos I'm from South America doesn't mean I'm a prostitute.

PATRICIA
I didn't plan on paying you.

MARIA
If I wanna stand, I stand. I'm not shy. I've done stuff with women, ok?

PATRICIA
I've had a really good night.

MARIA
Yeah me too. Not *really good*, but...

PATRICIA
You came back to mine.

MARIA
Like I said. I'm curious.

PATRICIA
You're curious about me?

MARIA
You don't like to smile, but you're not sad. I don't know, I thought that was... something.

PATRICIA
Would you sit down if I drink with you?

MARIA
You got ice?

PATRICIA
No.

MARIA
Must have a nice job to get an apartment in this area.

PATRICIA
It's not *that* nice a job. It's just work.

MARIA
Yeah but you're not a cleaner.

PATRICIA
You could do it for me?

MARIA

Oh, what, because of where I'm from now I'm a maid, is that it? First a prostitute now a maid. I guess I'm a thieving maid too: stealing the candlesticks and fucking all the men.

PATRICIA

At the bar you said you were a cleaner? I must have misheard.

MARIA

I'm kidding, relax. I was messing with you. You work central?

PATRICIA

I work all over. Not just in London. The Midlands, Sheffield.

MARIA

Manchester United. My brother loves Manchester United.

PATRICIA

You *do* know Manchester United isn't a city?

MARIA

Excuse me? Yes I know Manchester fucking United is not a city. Are you for real?

PATRICIA

I was joking this time.

An air of tension.

PATRICIA
I feel like maybe we should start again.

MARIA
I'm not some dumb fucking immigrant, but most of all–

MARIA pulls another bottle out from between her breasts.

MARIA
I am not shy.

PATRICIA
I thought you only had one.

MARIA smiles.

MARIA
What you do then? To have money for this expensive shithole?

PATRICIA
I work in credit.

MARIA
In a bank.

PATRICIA
It's not interesting.

MARIA
I want to know. You work with money.

PATRICIA
I work with people. I work *for* money.

MARIA
You're funny, for a girl who has a face like a slapped ass.

PATRICIA
I do not.

MARIA
This is your face, when you think nobody is watching you.

MARIA pulls a straight face.

MARIA
And you when you're listening.

MARIA pulls a subtly different face.

MARIA
I think it's cute, don't worry.

PATRICIA leans in and kisses MARIA, who pulls away and stands up.

PATRICIA
You said you've been with women? Is that like one... two?

MARIA
I've not finished asking you about your work.

PATRICIA
There really isn't anything...

MARIA
Yes, I know. You don't want to tell me what you do, so I'm guessing it's... something bad? You're in money, but not a bank... You... give those nasty loans to people who haven't got the cash to pay back? I'm right aren't you? You're the guy who kicks mothers and kids out on the street. No surprise you can't smile. Your soul must be blacker than coal. (*Beat*) Either that, or you just work with numbers all day, and you don't see nobody: you just move money from this pile to that pile, that pile to this. A life destroyed there, a business closed down here. I'm not judging, by the way, I'm just not seeing expensive jewellery...

PATRICIA
I put my earnings away.

MARIA
You must have some dark hobbies? Pot? Those silly eggs covered in gems and crap? *Fabergé*.

Beat.

PATRICIA
What do you do?

MARIA
I'm a cleaner.

PATRICIA

So you *are* a cleaner? I thought you said / I was racist for suggesting

MARIA

Ok ok, alright, yes, you were right. But it's just a job, it's not my entire life. Just for now, for cash.

PATRICIA

What did you do before? You said at the restaurant you lived in the US for a while?

MARIA

Really there's nothing to say. Why aren't we drunk? I feel myself getting more sober every second.

MARIA crouches.

PATRICIA

I don't really like vodka, if I'm honest.

MARIA

Vodka is not to *like*. It's just to make us more relaxed. To get you to smile. Lubrication.

MARIA sits.

PATRICIA

Is that flirting, or are you just being foreign?

PATRICIA touches MARIA's knee.

MARIA (*Quiet intensity*)
I think you're already a little drunk, or I hope so, because I do not fuck racists.

PATRICIA reaches her hand to MARIA's face. MARIA bites PATRICIA's hand. PATRICIA pulls her hand away in pain.

MARIA
A glass, for me and you. Or do you drink water straight from the tap?

PATRICIA stands up, blows on her bitten hand. She gives MARIA a look, then exits.
Beat. MARIA takes a small vile from her pocket. She unscrews the lid and uses a pipette to drip some of the contents into one of the vodka bottles. The sound of smashing offstage- MARIA spills some of the liquid. Urgently she wipes up the spillage with her dress, and hides the vile.

Enter PATRICIA holding a broken handmade mug.

PATRICIA
I broke my only cup.

MARIA stands and offers PATRICIA the spiked vodka. She takes it.

MARIA
To lubrication.

MARIA and PATRICIA drink their vodkas. PATRICIA goes to kiss MARIA. MARIA pulls away to avoid contact with the lips.

PATRICIA
Alright what's going on?

MARIA's eyes momentarily glance at PATRICIA's vodka bottle. PATRICIA frowns, looks at the bottle, suspicious.

MARIA
Ok maybe I am shy, alright?

PATRICIA
I mean, you swiped right-

MARIA
You messaged me.

PATRICIA
Do you want to fuck, yes or no?

MARIA
I thought you looked nice. Like a good person.

PATRICIA
Well that was your error.

MARIA
So are you the man-woman, or the woman-woman?

PATRICIA
Are you being serious? I'm your first, aren't I?

MARIA
Ok, maybe I've not. Maybe you are my first, maybe... Maybe I've just had enough of men for a bit. Wanted a holiday, I dunno.

PATRICIA
"Holiday". Thanks.

MARIA
Look, I don't know what I'm doing ok, I'm not gay, or curious, I'm just me, ok? I'm just this.

PATRICIA
Same. Good.

MARIA
Fucking excellent.

PATRICIA
So you clearly need some help with this: step one- there isn't a man-woman and a woman-woman.

MARIA
You gonna be angry the whole time?

PATRICIA
As long as you act like a prick, yes.

MARIA
You should smile more.

PATRICIA is woozy.

PATRICIA
I thought the... the restaurant was nice. I was having a good time- feel a bit. My stomach. It doesn't matter. You're funny, ok. And I'm sorry and I think you're very funny. I want to laugh. I want you to make me laugh.

MARIA
I used to be a comedian, you know? In Colombia. Not for a long time. Just before I had to leave, only for about six months. But I was good.

PATRICIA
Why did you... stop?

MARIA
Because nobody wants a Colombian comedian in America.

PATRICIA
Why... not? Just... translate the... jokes.

MARIA
I tried that, it isn't funny.

PATRICIA
I want to. I want t-t-to hear one. Tell me a Colombian joke... in English.

MARIA
Nah, it loses it's feeling in English. It's all in the way you say it.

PATRICIA
I want to laugh / though.

MARIA
Ok, I'll try, but promise not to laugh. Ok, no, you know what I mean. It won't be funny.

PATRICIA (*Getting woozier*)
I'm... all ears.

MARIA
Alright... A nun walks into church, and donkey is nailed to a cross, and the nun says... No, I'm not going to even... You see. English it's like the people here. It is a depressed language. Spanish... it is funny even if you don't try. English is like everybody is already depressed. Especially in London. Everyone talks like they love the floor. Have some pride people, *god*.

PATRICIA lies back on the sheet, head resting on the pillow.

PATRICIA
I think the vodka...

MARIA watches PATRICIA pass out. Satisfied she is asleep, MARIA checks around the apartment for any valuables.

MARIA checks under the pillow and finds a knife. She looks at it, then PATRICIA. Lights down.

Tom and the EmotiPiece

TOM presses the button on his new watch. It releases a compressed shot of synthetic Oxytocin into his bloodstream. He smiles. After a moment, he does it again. TOM keeps pressing the button again and again.

Somebody is Better Than Nobody

PATRICIA wakes up. MARIA is sat at the end of the sheets, reading a letter. She is holding PATRICIA's knife. PATRICIA recoils, afraid, catching MARIA's attention.

MARIA
This is today.

PATRICIA
Wha... wha, what. What happened- how did? I don't...

MARIA
I want to come with you.

PATRICIA
Did you... you did something. To the drink.

MARIA holds the letter up.

MARIA
Nobody should go alone to this.

PATRICIA feels around for the knife.

MARIA
Now I know why you have this under your pillow.

MARIA holds out the knife.

PATRICIA
Take what you want, ok. I, I... have money, I-

MARIA
I don't want your money. I want to go to the meeting.

PATRICIA
I'm not going... and even if I was. Why would I let you come?

MARIA
Because somebody is better than nobody.

PATRICIA
You don't know me. You don't know anything about me.

MARIA
Maybe not everything, but *some*thing. And you can trust me.

PATRICIA
You drugged me.

MARIA
Yes, but it's the morning and I'm still here.

Beat.

PATRICIA
Can you put my knife down?

MARIA
Of course.

MARIA passes PATRICIA the knife. PATRICIA instantly threatens MARIA with it.

PATRICIA
Why did you spike my drink?

MARIA
So I could rob you. You didn't have anything worth taking. I put your money back in your purse.

PATRICIA
Don't pretend you care.

MARIA
I'm not pretending.

PATRICIA
I will cut you.

MARIA
Did *he* have a knife? This...

MARIA holds the letter up.

MARIA
This ass / hole

PATRICIA
Put my stuff down and get out of my flat.

MARIA
My cousin, he raped me. I was just a kid. I didn't know it was rape cos I loved him very much and he did it with my sisters, so. I thought it was ok: we all did. He was much older than us this big man... I think I thought I loved him, but. I think I was just scared? When my dad found out- he kicked me out. That's when I first moved, to Bogota, from our village. I hated that city and I loved it, but it was there I grew into myself, learned about the world, my body. But I was never happy. I've always had lovers... that was easy for me. I just went for it, and even after, in America and here I guess too. It's just what I do best. I've never been paid for it, I never allowed myself to do that. Too many girls I grew up with have gone that way. I've had many lovers, but... friends. That isn't easy for me, to trust. I've always had that night when I was 12 on me, like the weight of a body: his body. But you, I trust. You don't have to believe me, but you- I know why your eyes have wrinkles. I have the same

sleepless nights and the same bad dreams. I regret a lot of things in my life, but coming with you to meet this man is not going to be one. I think it might be the best thing I will ever do.

Tom is Too Happy

Tom lies on the floor, his body shaking in seizure.

Complete Lifeness

ACORN is sat serenely. MARIA paces about. PATRICIA stands still, studying ACORN. Beat.

MARIA
Are you gonna let him stare at you like that? (*Beat*) Sorry.

PATRICIA
He doesn't look like I remember. (*Beat*) I don't know if... I don't think it's him.

MARIA
People all change.

PATRICIA
No. It's not him.

MARIA
It was dark, probably, anyway, no? Or he covered his face, or yours?

PATRICIA
I'm going to go.

MARIA
Don't. Look... Sorry. I won't ask you about it, but. You're here now.

PATRICIA
I don't know what I thought this would do.

MARIA (*To ACORN*)
Asshole, stop staring at us. Asshole. Don't think cos they're watching that I won't break you.

PATRICIA
He didn't cover his face. When he attacked me. The man, he didn't... I saw his face. This man is... I don't know who this is.

MARIA
Our memories twist faces. Plays with what we remember.

PATRICIA
I remember his face, Maria. Don't you think I remember?

Beat.

MARIA
The police say this is him.

PATRICIA turns back to ACORN, who has been watching the two of them the whole time, barely moving, with a subtle smile on his face.

MARIA
Asshole. You remember her, no? You remember this woman. (*Beat*) I'm talking to you. (*Beat*) You fucking talk or what?

ACORN
I talk.

MARIA
Well talk then. I asked you a question.

ACORN
I don't remember your friend.

PATRICIA
Can we go now?

MARIA
No, I'm not buying that. Five years ago you attacked this woman. (*Beat*) No, nothing?

ACORN
I am not what I did.

PATRICIA
What?

ACORN
The man Michael John McDonnell may have attacked you, but that man is dead. I am Acorn.

MARIA
Acorn?

PATRICIA
Just... please. (*To ACORN*) What do you mean "I am not what I did?"

Beat.

ACORN
Each nightfall I die, every sunrise I am reborn. Today, I am ACORN. The man who attacked you is long dead.

MARIA
He's... insane.

PATRICIA
Can I just. Do you remember me, though? You remember my face?

ACORN
Acorn neither remembers, nor forgets. He exists in a state of nowness, of complete lifeness. His threads neither reach forwards nor backwards but tie him to the moment.

PATRICIA
Five years ago, in August, I was walking through Hampstead Heath. A man grabbed me from behind and took me

into a wooded area. He gagged me, tied my arms, and raped me, whilst looking in my eyes. Every time I closed mine he pulled them open, so I saw him, so I couldn't help but look into his cold, empty, hollow eyes.

ACORN
My form is transient. Consciousness is being-

MARIA
Give me the nod and I will rip the life out of this man, Patricia. If you don't, I will: I don't care what happens, just give me the sign.

PATRICIA
Let him talk. (*To ACORN*) Who are you, then? If you aren't this man they say you are.

ACORN
Today I am ACORN.

MARIA
And yesterday? Pinecone?

ACORN
Acorn does not hold on to the past self. The past has passed, that's why they call it the past!

PATRICIA
They said you're on a hunger strike.

ACORN
I am not "on strike".

PATRICIA
Do you feel like you were wrongly arrested?

Long beat.

MARIA
You were right, Patricia. We should go. There's no sense from this man. He's sick.

PATRICIA
It's an act, Maria. Psychologists have done tests. He's just lying to protect himself.

MARIA
I don't know how they can let him do this.

PATRICIA
He knows what he did. (*To ACORN*) If you don't regret, what *do* you feel? You must feel something.

ACORN
I feel only life.

MARIA
What do you know about life? How dare you feel anything but shame.

ACORN
Shame is illusory. It is a backward projection.

PATRICIA
So you're just... alive?

ACORN
It is the only thing anyone can feel if one is truly open to the universe.

MARIA
So you're a fucking Buddhist, well done. Just to be clear: if there's a hell, Hitler's saving you a seat.

ACORN
I am a Jainist, and as such, I do not follow the belief that Heaven or Hell exist, rather that salvation is achieved through perfection over many lives. I pray, I tend to my plants, I allow my *self* to emerge not from within, but without. I absorb the world and my mind goes with it. I am air in my lungs, I am blood in my veins, I am water-

MARIA
You're a rapist.

Beat.

ACORN
Acorn cannot regret because Acorn has no past, and because Acorn has no future, Acorn cannot pine.

PATRICIA starts to laugh, genuinely, from deep inside her self. She can't stop. She laughs and laughs. MARIA doesn't know how to react. ACORN is his usual serene self. PATRICIA's laugh keeps coming, growing to a tearful wheeze. MARIA catches the bug and starts laughing too. They laugh together boisterously at ACORN's absurdity, and though they often reach the cusp of forming sentences, they are never able to break the spell of the laughter long enough to enunciate. ACORN grows uncomfortable.

ACORN (*Uncertain*)
Guards?

An Answer

GEORGE inspects CLOWNIER's body. It has grown rigid. He shoos a fly away. It comes back, and lands on CLOWNIER's face. GEORGE slaps CLOWNIER's face to kill the fly, but the fly escapes. GEORGE regrets slapping CLOWNIER's face so hard. He stands her up and hugs her.

With effort, GEORGE repositions CLOWNIER's arms so he is able to dance with her to the hold music. At the height of the routine, he pirouettes her outwards, at which moment, the call centre answer his call.

PHONE
Hello, thank you for holding-

GEORGE rushes to the PHONE, losing control of CLOWNIER, who slams to the floor like a plank. GEORGE winces at his own clumsiness.

PHONE (*Concerned by the noise*)
Are you... ok?

GEORGE (*Earnest*)
Yes.

PHONE
Ok, great, can I start by taking *your* name, please?

GEORGE
My name, or-

PHONE
Yes, your name please.

GEORGE
George Clowny.

Beat.

PHONE
Can you repeat that?

GEORGE
George. Clowny.

Curtain.

---------------------------*END* ---------------------------

About the Playwrights & Theatre

Rachel O'Regan is a Scotland-based playwright. Rachel's first full-length play Hungerland won a Bread and Roses Playwriting Award in 2019. In 2021, her play Afterparty, with F-Bomb Theatre, sold out its entire run at Edinburgh Fringe. She also has a Playwriting MFA from Edinburgh Napier University.

Darren Donohue is an award-winning Irish poet and playwright. His plays are produced internationally with Irish Repertory Theatre (New York), the Keegan Theatre (Washington DC), Piccolo Teatro (Milan), and Bread and Roses Theatre (London). His work garnered a number of awards including the Radius Playwriting Prize, in association with Finborough Theatre.

Hugh Dichmont is a Nottingham-based writer. Plays include The War On Terry (UK tour), Pareidolia (Catalyst Festival), and short works at Theatre 503, Old Red Lion Theatre, the Pleasance and The Vaults. *www.hugh-dichmont.com*

The Bread & Roses Theatre is an intimate and versatile fringe venue that boasts a wide variety of productions which bring in local and far-reaching audiences alike. Artistic quality and representation of our societies' real diversity are at the heart of the theatre's programming with a focus on new writing, underrepresented voices, distinctive work and the development of new work and opportunities.

The Bread & Roses Theatre
68 Clapham Manor Street, London SW4 6DZ
www.breadandrosestheatre.co.uk

www.ingramcontent.com/pod-product-compliance
Lightning Source LLC
Chambersburg PA
CBHW071724080526
44588CB00013B/1888